M000317142

ELIZABETH AND RICH K
Our Travel Menu (www.ou
approach' to travelling the world. They have been sharing their
passion for travel since they met on a business trip in Hawaii in 2006
and have explored over 50 countries across 6 continents together.
They decided to pursue their dream to travel the world for a year and
wrote the book, *The Couple's Guide To World Travel*, to help others
to realize their own travel dreams.

THE COUPLE'S GUIDE TO WORLD TRAVEL

Dream it, Plan it, Love it

ELIZABETH AND RICH KERIAN

TO: DAWN & JOE,
HAPPY TRAVELS!
Rich Kerian
Elizabeth Kerian

SilverWood

ISBN 978-0-9998669-0-0 (paperback)
ISBN 978-0-9998669-1-7 (ebook)

British Library Cataloguing in Publication Data
A CIP catalogue record for this book is available from the British Library

Page design and typesetting by SilverWood Books
www.silverwoodbooks.co.uk

Printed on responsibly sourced paper

Table of Contents

Acknowledgements

We have many, many people whom we've never met to thank for their knowledge and inspiration. We took advantage of various travel blogs, forums, articles, websites, books, TV shows, podcasts, and more. We met travelers along the way who helped us make spontaneous decisions to alter course and visit magnificent places that we otherwise would not have experienced. We also benefited from so many fellow travelers who took the time to post their experiences on websites such as www.tripadvisor.com. We make numerous references throughout this book to the resources that we used, and we try our best to give credit where credit is due. That said, it's impossible for us to individually thank these people. Instead, we have made an effort to share our knowledge by maintaining our free travel blog at www.ourtravelmenu.com as a resource and by posting our own reviews on travel sites as appropriate. We hope that we can pass along to others, like yourself, some travel knowledge and information that may help inspire you the way those that have gone before us have inspired us. We'd also like to thank our copy editor Sherry Roberts for all of her efforts (www.editorialservice.com).

The Amuse Bouche

Introduction

Preface

If you've ever dreamed of traveling the world with your spouse or partner and wondered how to do it, this book is for you. We tell the story of how we turned our passion for travel into a year-long trip around the world. And, then we provide the recipe for how you can make your own trip. Consider this a practical guide for couples to plan and take an extended travel adventure together. Perhaps you're young and considering a gap year, or maybe you're approaching retirement and wondering what you're going to do with yourselves. A year may be too long or too costly. No worries, our menu approach to world travel can be easily adapted to any time frame and lets you pick and choose what appeals to your tastes and your budget.

While we cover destinations that we visited to provide context, our focus is more about how to do it rather than where to go. Consider our travels to be an appetizer that precedes your main course. We provide tips, tricks, resources, and tools that we've used effectively. Along the way, we share our experiences to take the mystery out of what life on the road is really like. And you might even get a chuckle or two out of the anecdotes that we relate. More than anything else, it is our sincere wish that our story might provide inspiration to others to turn their travel dreams into reality. If we could do it, so can you.

The first section of the book relates the story of *what we did*. This will give you some background on us and our approach to travel. The next section gives you deep insight into how to *plan and prepare* for time off traveling the world to see and experience the places that have most captured your imagination. Finally, you'll learn how you and your significant other can *survive on the road* to achieve your very own personal travel dreams. Like any good recipe, we provide the ingredients and directions that worked well for us. However, like any good chef, we encourage you to improvise and modify the recipe to suit your own personal tastes and needs.

What this book is not. While we tell our story and mention places that we've visited, we're not trying to influence where you travel. We've already thoroughly documented our travels on our travel blog, which can be found at www.ourtravelmenu.com. There are many other resources that can spark your interest on where to visit. However, when it comes to planning an extended travel adventure, it's difficult to find a comprehensive guide that provides you with everything you need to know. We had to piece ideas and advice together from the experiences of others and then teach ourselves along the way. You can benefit from our experiences and avoid the mistakes we made (like getting deported in Finland, more on that later). If you yearn for an extended travel adventure but feel overwhelmed by the logistics associated with such a trip, you've come to the right place. We'll take the mystery out of world travel and help you figure out how to start down your own path as a world traveler.

So, let's get started with our story.

Our Story

The Fantasy

We met in Hawaii while we were attending the same business meeting, but representing different companies. Each of our jobs required that we travel frequently for business. A few of the attendees in Hawaii liked to run for exercise. So, several of us planned an early morning group run one day. As fate would have it, we were the only ones who showed up. While Rich tried to keep up with Elizabeth's energetic pace, we got to know each other a little better and the seeds of a relationship that would blossom over time were sown.

At the time, Elizabeth lived in Chicago and Rich in New Jersey. We kept in touch and looked for opportunities where our business travel plans might coincide. The next time we met was a few months later at a conference in Phoenix, Arizona. The conference ended early on the final day, and we headed to Sedona for an afternoon of hiking. Sedona is well known for its beautiful red rock formations. The locals claim that there are a number of "energy vortexes" located there. We selected one named Bell Rock as the destination for our hike. The hike itself is fairly easy, but it took some effort to climb about 150 feet up the rock formation where we found a comfortable place to sit and chat while we admired the beautiful scenery that surrounded us.

While we were sitting there, we started to pinpoint travel

destinations that we'd like to visit. Wouldn't it be nice if we could visit California wine country together? Or, how about the Grand Canyon? Or, maybe Las Vegas? How about Florida during the wintertime? Over the next several months, we had a lot of fun planning and turning those fantasy trips into a reality.

Little did Rich know that Elizabeth had set her sights on going back to school to pursue an MBA, and she was especially interested in expanding her horizons by studying abroad. She applied to the University College Dublin Michael Smurfit Graduate Business School in Ireland and was accepted. After about six months of fantasy travel, Rich realized that Elizabeth would be leaving for Ireland to begin her studies in about three months.

The relationship could have ended there, but Rich made several trips to Ireland to visit Elizabeth and our fantasy travels expanded internationally. We also took advantage of her spring break to venture Down Under and attend the wedding of a close friend of Elizabeth's in Australia, a country that we quickly fell in love with.

Rich somehow persuaded Elizabeth to come back to the USA upon the completion of her studies and move in with him at the Jersey shore. Elizabeth decided to pursue her passion for wine and began her career anew in the wine and spirits industry. Little did we know that this would eventually have a heavy influence on our future travel destinations. Our new home base in New Jersey became a convenient launching pad for numerous short-term trips to Europe with some of our favorite destinations being Norway, Switzerland, and Spain. The more places we traveled to, the more our appetite for additional international travel grew.

Even though Elizabeth had successfully completed her MBA program in the summer, the degrees were not bestowed until the following spring. We travelled together to Dublin to attend the graduation. A few days before the ceremony, Rich proposed during an encore visit to the lovely Powerscourt House and Gardens. We were happily married the following year in Columbia, Missouri, where Elizabeth grew up.

Going Global

By now, you've probably figured out that we like to travel. It was not uncommon for us to take a trip once a month. Sometimes it would be a domestic trip and sometimes it would be an international trip. Every now and then, we would fantasize and wonder what it would be like to travel the world for a year. The idea held a lot of appeal, but we didn't have any role models to follow and it seemed unrealistic. Then, one day, the publicly traded company that Rich worked for was taken private. A number of employees, including Rich, were offered equity-like opportunities in the business that might pay out handsomely in approximately five years as long as the company was successful and Rich was still employed there. We decided that this was our big chance. If Rich could make it to "exit" as they call it when the private equity firm sold the company, we might have enough money to take a year off and travel the world.

We now had a plan with a faint light of hope at the end of the tunnel. However, the severe financial crisis that subsequently damaged the US economy had a trickle-down effect that included the company Rich worked for. Three and a half years after the company was taken private, Rich's position was eliminated. There would be no windfall to fund our world travel fantasy.

While Rich was now out of work, he did receive a severance package, which sparked an idea. He soon started lobbying

Elizabeth to quit her job and travel the world with him until his severance ran out. Elizabeth was torn. She had just been promoted into a dream job and was eager to prove herself. Being pragmatic, we realized that we really weren't prepared yet to drop everything and head off on a world travel adventure. We decided that Rich would try to find another job and we would start saving in earnest to take a year off to travel the world. The sooner he found a job, the sooner we could start banking his severance toward the trip. In the meantime, Elizabeth would gain valuable experience in her new job role. Fortunately, Rich was able to land a consulting gig, and we agreed that when our lease was up in a year, that's when we would begin our year-long adventure.

Now we had a goal but, in truth, it was still just talk. After several more months passed by, we decided that if we were truly serious, then we needed to *put a stake in the ground* to make it real. We had accumulated quite a few frequent traveler points from all of our personal and business travel. So, in December, we used some of our points to book a one-way ticket to Beijing, China at the end of August in the following year. This gave us eight more months to save, plan, and prepare. Now, it was game on. We had a goal to go global.

Our Travel Menu

Now that we had a departure date, the clock was ticking. We started our travel planning with a few simple *guiding principles*. First, we wanted to *stay warm* by avoiding winter. Second, we wanted to *be flexible* in our planning so that we could make spontaneous travel decisions along the journey. That way, if we liked a place, we could extend our stay and vice versa. We were also hoping that we'd meet fellow travelers along the trip who would influence our travel destinations based on their travel experiences.

Given the fact that we would be leaving on August 31 coupled with our desire to *stay warm*, we were able to map out a general plan that would keep us in the Northern Hemisphere for the first couple of months of autumn, then we'd drop down into the Southern Hemisphere where it would be late spring and stay through their summer (our winter) before resurfacing in the Northern Hemisphere for spring and summer. Since we had already booked the first leg of our trip to China, we decided that we would start out in Asia, then move down into Oceania, across to South America, across again to Africa, and finish up north in Europe.

Even though we had an outline for our trip, we still wanted to *stay flexible* within the outline. Neither one of us is very good at cooking, and after our usual long days at work, we also lacked the ambition to cook a meal. So, we often would go out to dinner. One day when we were browsing the menu trying to decide what we'd like to order, a light bulb of sorts went off: Why don't we take a menu approach to our travel? Thus, the *travel menu* became our third guiding principle. We would prepare a list of places we'd like to visit, and we'd make choices along the way just like we do when we go out to eat. We subsequently leveraged this principle to come up with the name for the travel blog where we documented our travel experiences: www.ourtravelmenu.com.

Prep Time

Looking back, we're really glad that we had a lot of time to prepare for our trip. We used the time to not only consider where we wanted to go, but we also needed to figure out things like luggage, clothing, visas, immunizations, and the like. It also gave us time to save up as much money and as many travel points as we could.

We made a list of all of the things that we could think of that we needed to take care of and then we scoured the Internet for everything we could find. We became human sponges soaking up all the information that we could get our hands on. There are a lot of great free resources out there, if you can find them. It took considerable time and effort, which we can save you with our guidance in this book.

As the months passed by and our launch date moved ever closer, we had to start making decisions on what to do with all of our stuff. We lived in a one-bedroom apartment in Hoboken, New Jersey, just across the Hudson River from New York City. We thought about putting our stuff into storage, but that comes at a price and the money that we'd save if we didn't pay for storage could be used to buy new things upon our return. We also were unsure of where we'd want to live when we got back. We were pretty certain that we wanted to come back to the USA. However, if ever there was a good time to select a new location to call home, it would be at the end of our trip. Thus, we made the decision to purge most of what we owned.

Bon Voyage

Since we weren't going to see our friends and family for a year, we made a point of seeing as many of them as we could before we left. Next, it was just a matter of wrapping up the final details. We finished up work and turned in any company equipment that we had acquired. We placed our wedding rings in a safe deposit box and replaced them with simple inexpensive ones. We set up our mail for forwarding to Elizabeth's parents. We contacted our credit and debit card companies to notify them that we'd be traveling abroad for a year. We had our mobile phones "unlocked" so that we could use them with international SIM cards. And, on and on. Don't worry, we provide a detailed checklist of all the little details that need to be taken care of later in the book.

We arranged it so that we departed on the last day of the month when our lease was up. We emptied our apartment, hoisted our backpacks, and dropped off the apartment keys at the reception desk in the lobby. We met the prearranged car service to take us to Newark Liberty International Airport. We had checked in online the day before and didn't have any bags to check. So, we headed for security followed by immigration control.

While we planned to be budget-minded throughout our trip, we started off with perhaps our biggest splurge—we flew first-class nonstop from Newark to Beijing. We did this for a few reasons. First, it was a great deal. It would have cost over $5,000 apiece to purchase these tickets, which is inconceivable for us to pay. However, we had amassed hundreds of thousands of United MileagePlus points, and the tickets would only cost us 70,000 points apiece. The equivalent economy ticket cost approximately $900 or 35,000 points. So, it seemed like a great deal. Second, we wanted to have something really exciting to look forward to that would help prevent us from changing our start date. We'd been fortunate enough to fly business class on a long-distance flight before but never first class. So, we used our miles for a once-in-a-lifetime indulgence. We left the USA on Saturday, August 31, and arrived in China on Sunday, September 1. Needless to say, it was quite a treat.

Now that we've given you some background on how we planned our trip, it's time for you to begin planning your trip. At the end of each section, we'll highlight the key ingredients that you should consider.

Key Ingredients

Consider the following ideas to get started:

- Draft a general plan – Ours was to travel the world for a year and stay warm. We would start out in Asia, move down into Oceania, then over to South America, followed by Africa, and finish up in Europe.
- Take time to prepare – We gave ourselves more than eight months to get ready.
- Put a stake in the ground – In December, we booked a flight to Beijing, China, departing the following August 31.

Appetizers

Planning

Gaining Inspiration and Setting Goals

There are many questions that you and your companion will want to ask yourselves in the initial stages of planning an extended international trip:

- What countries do we want to visit?
- Where should we start?
- How long would we like to be away?
- How much can we afford to spend? Do we have a budget?
- What are the places we absolutely can't miss?
- How long will we stay in each place?
- What type of accommodations are we going to stay in?
- Do we need to have everything thoroughly planned in advance or are we willing to be spontaneous?

The list of questions can become quite extensive and a bit overwhelming. No worries. We aim to help you answer these questions and some additional ones that you probably haven't even thought of yet.

We began to gather ideas on the places that we'd like to visit. The ideas came from various sources: *National Geographic Traveler Magazine* and similar periodicals, suggestions from friends and family about their favorite travel destinations, TV shows such as Anthony Bourdain's entertaining *No Reservations* and *Parts Unknown*, and podcasts such as Chris Christensen's incredible *Amateur Traveler* series (http://amateurtraveler.com) and Gary Bembridge's *Tips for Travellers* (www.tipsfortravellers.com). Chris does a great job of interviewing people about different places around the world, while Gary talks a lot about his own personal experiences. They both inspired us to add places to our list that we wouldn't have otherwise. To gain further inspiration and motivation, we also encourage you to visit the blog from our trip at www.ourtravelmenu.com to see if there are any additional places of interest for you and your partner. As we accumulated ideas, we started logging them in a document that was organized by continent. We would add a country that we would like to visit and then list the places of interest that caught our attention within that country.

We often found ideas while browsing the Internet. We created a browser bookmark folder named "World Travel" and then used subfolders to keep it organized. We named one of the subfolders "Places to Visit" and bookmarked sites of interest in this folder. An example of one such site is www.climate-zone.com. We used this site to get a better sense of what the weather would be like at different times of the year. This helped us think about how we might sequence visiting the areas of the world that we were interested in.

We also started to read some books on travel destinations to gather more ideas for our travel menu and to gain some insights into foreign culture and history. One such example is *Wild Swans* by Jung Chang. This fascinating story provided perspective on the hardships of life in China during the twentieth century. The historical information provided in the book gave us an appreciation for some of the regional hostilities that still exist today among Asian countries. Learning such things in advance of our trip better prepared us for our visits. A couple of other books that inspired us were:

- Lonely Planet's *The Travel Book—A Journey Through Every Country in the World.*
- *1,000 Places to See Before You Die* by Patricia Schultz.

Key Ingredients

Gaining Inspiration And Setting Goals:

- Gather ideas on places that you'd like to visit and start logging them by continent and country (check out Appendix B to see our original list).
- Read periodicals such as *National Geographic Traveler.*
- Visit your local library to browse through travel books and periodicals.
- Ask friends and family what their favorite travel destinations have been.
- Watch TV shows such as Anthony Bourdain's *No Reservations* and *Parts Unknown.*
- Listen to podcasts such as Chris Christensen's *Amateur Traveler* series.
- Read books to learn more about the history and culture of places you're visiting.

Saving Up

We recommend establishing a separate bank account dedicated to saving for your trip. This makes it easy to track your progress. We took it one step further and opened up a brokerage account and invested some of our savings in the stock market. This is risky as you can lose money this way. Whether you go down a similar path or not will depend upon your risk tolerance. If you're wondering how much the trip cost us, we provide the details later in the "How Much is Enough?" chapter. In addition to cash, we recommend that you start accumulating travel reward points as described below.

Earn Points for Travel with Credit Card Deals

Credit cards offer creative ways to save up for your trip. There are many credit card offers in which you can earn significant bonus points just by meeting the minimum spending requirements. Once we met the requirements for one card, we would move onto another one to keep gathering up points. If the card had an annual fee, we would cancel it after we earned the up-front bonus and before the annual fee hit. Two great online resources to get started on deciding which card or cards are best for you are www.extrapackofpeanuts.com and www.thepointsguy.com. Both of these sites keep up-to-date posts on the cards that give you the best point deals.

As an example, we each signed up for an IHG Rewards card from Chase that earned us 60,000 bonus points apiece after we each spent $1,000 within the first three months. IHG stands for International Hotel Group and includes brands such as Intercontinental, Holiday Inn, Crowne Plaza, and more. The best part is that every two months, IHG posts its "PointBreaks" awards where it offers properties around the world for just 5,000 points per night, which is an incredible deal. After spending a total of $2,000 on everyday things that we needed anyway, we had 122,000 IHG points that gave us the potential to obtain twenty-four free hotel rooms during our trip. You may find this hard to believe, but when we left for our trip, we had amassed over two million hotel and airline points through business travel, personal travel, and credit card bonuses. Not only did this save us a ton of money on our trip, we got to stay in some luxurious hotels for free such as the Park Hyatt in Seoul, which we never would have paid for on our own.

While speaking about credit cards, it's important to understand what fees are charged by both credit and debit card issuers. There are big disparities among various cards. If you are travelling abroad, you will want to make sure that your cards charge zero transaction fees for foreign currency exchange and that you don't get dinged for ATM bank fees. In addition, you may want to make sure your credit cards provide rental car insurance protection so you don't have to keep paying for it when you rent cars. Fortunately, there are many credit cards to choose from, just be sure to take a close look at the fine print when figuring out which cards will accompany you on your trip.

We recommend that you each take two credit cards and two debit cards that are different from each other. Then, one person can carry one of the credit cards and debit cards while the other keeps theirs locked in their luggage. To keep track of all your cards and points, you may want to consider putting together a spreadsheet that includes the card information, phone numbers to call in the event the card is lost or stolen, and the date the renewal fees will be assessed. We suggest that you password protect and store it in the cloud. If you're not comfortable taking this risk, then come up with an alternative backup plan such as leaving this information with a family member. We provide a guide to keep track of this information in Appendix E along with a Reward Points tracking guide in Appendix F. Finally, we also stored backup cards with our parents so they could ship the cards to us in case of an emergency.

To further maximize our points, we used United MileagePlus's Shopping website to buy things that we needed. We bought nonperishable grocery items from Walmart, as an example, and met the minimum requirement so that they'd be shipped to our apartment for free. This earned us double points for each dollar we spent: one for using the shopping portal and one for using our current rewards credit card. And, it was incredibly convenient.

Banking and ATM Cards

We searched for a bank with a debit card that had no foreign transaction fees and didn't charge ATM fees. We found what we were looking for at Capital One. Its card has no foreign transaction fees and never charges an ATM fee on its side for using another bank's ATM. Capital One also rebates up to $15 per month of other banks' ATM fees. Our primary backup, an E*Trade debit card, never charged an ATM fee of any kind, but it did charge a 1 percent foreign transaction fee. Given that it was a backup card, we felt that we could live with it.

One final note on debit cards, we brought along both a Visa and a MasterCard debit card, and we were glad we did. Our primary debit card was a MasterCard. Much to our surprise, we found that most ATMs in Uganda only accepted Visa debit cards. Luckily, we had one. It might be a good idea for you to also carry one of each brand with you. We also found that once outside the USA, the ATM fees charged by foreign banks were not readily recognized by Capital One and therefore not automatically rebated. So, we would have to call the bank using Skype every couple of months and talk to customer service to get the foreign banks' fees rebated. It was a bit of a hassle, but we had the time and every little bit counts when you have no income.

Key Ingredients

Saving Up:

- Start saving your money.
- Save up travel points and acquire reward credit cards.
- Think about what credit and debit cards you'll want to take on the trip.
- Log all of your credit card information, including phone numbers to call if lost or stolen, in a spreadsheet that you password protect and store in the cloud (see our guide in Appendix E).
- Ask a family member or friend to hold at least one backup credit and debit card for you, which they can ship to you in case of emergency.
- Open a joint bank account with electronic bill paying if you don't already have one. This will become your primary banking account while on the trip. Ideally, one of your debit cards is tied to this account.

Preparing

Visas

The next thing that we focused on was visas. Most countries don't require special visas for US citizens, but some countries do and it can take a few weeks to acquire them. We provide details on how to find out whether a visa is required or not in the "Pre-Arrival" planning section. In addition, you need to make sure that your passports are in order. They need to have an expiration date that is at least six months longer than the last travel date you plan on. We both had plenty of runway on our passports so that was not a problem.

We also needed to have lots of empty passport pages for immigration stamps. Rich's passport was older than Elizabeth's and was running short of blank pages. So, Rich had to send his passport in and pay a fee to have additional pages added. We determined that we would need to acquire advance visas for China, India, and Russia. Upon further analysis, we learned that the Russian visa is only good for six months from the date of issue, and since we didn't plan to visit Russia until the tail end of our trip, it made no sense to obtain such a visa before we left. Visas are not cheap. Costing several hundred dollars, they're one of the unexpected costs of world travel that we encountered. Nevertheless, we paid the fees and obtained the necessary visas for both China and India. We used the services offered by www.travisa.com to obtain our visas, and we were pleased with the service that the company provided for the additional fees charged.

Immunizations/Prescriptions

We used the Centers for Disease Control and Prevention's excellent health and safety information website (www.cdc.gov/travel/) to do our homework on immunizations to determine if any were required and what other risks of disease we might face. On the CDC's website, for every country, you will find a section on "Vaccines and Medicines". Here they list the recommended vaccines and medicines they suggest getting prior to traveling to that country. We decided to get immunizations for yellow fever and hepatitis A and B.

Unfortunately, the hepatitis A and B immunization requires three shots over six months. We got the second shot at home just before we left. Halfway through our trip, we were in South Africa when it was time for the third and final shot. We made an appointment at a local travel clinic. We were thrilled when we finally left the doctor's office with all of our shots now behind us. It's also worth noting that the cost of immunization in South Africa was about a third of what we paid in the USA.

In addition to immunizations, we needed to get a prescription for anti-malaria medication. There are a few medications to choose from with various effectiveness, side effects, dosages, and costs. We chose Malarone, which requires daily dosages when needed. We ended up purchasing ninety pills to take with us to share, which turned out to be more than enough for our travel destinations. We actually only used the medication for our safari in Africa. We had to start the meds one week before our arrival in Uganda and continue taking them for another week after our departure. Aside from experiencing some really weird dreams that can result from the medication, it served us well. If you think that there's a chance that you might end up in a country where you'll face a risk of malaria, we recommend that you play it safe and get a prescription filled before you leave so that you're well prepared.

Health Insurance

To the best of our knowledge, most domestic health insurance plans do not provide international coverage. Ours did not. We searched the Internet and found some plans that provided coverage that included emergency evacuation transportation back to the US, if necessary (e.g., www.worldnomads.com). We weren't concerned with paying for routine medical and dental care, and we felt that we could cover local emergency transportation costs if need be. Our concern was to protect against something catastrophic such as if one or both of us was in a serious accident. So, we sought out a policy that we hoped we'd never need and that we didn't expect to reimburse us unless something really awful happened to one of us. We found just what we were looking for with GeoBlue. We selected a GeoBlue Xplorer plan with a $2,500 deductible that provided the catastrophic coverage we were looking for. It cost us $412 per month for both of us and only provided coverage outside of the United States. Thus, we spent approximately $5,000 on health insurance that we never used. That's a lot of money, but it provided us with peace of mind and it's hard to put a price tag on that. You should evaluate whether any existing health insurance coverage that you have could be extended to provide international coverage for you and your partner. If not, you should determine what type of coverage makes sense for you and see what international health insurance plans are available, such as GeoBlue. Then select one and apply for coverage. Please note that the application and underwriting process can be time-consuming. You'll want to apply 60-90 days before you leave to be on the safe side.

Technology

We can't imagine how we would have traveled the world as we did for so long without the wonderful technology that accompanied us. We reference our devices throughout the book. Here we'll provide a little more insight into the technology that we used.

We are fans of Apple products, and so, most of the technology we brought along was made by Apple. We are not saying that you have to use these devices; this is just our personal preference, and they served us well. We'll start with our notebook. We took just one, which we shared. It was a thirteen-inch MacBook Air that weighed about three pounds. Its sleek design made it easy for Rich to slip it in and out of his backpack. Our model had a 256GB flash drive for storage. This was enough to meet our needs, but Rich did keep an eye on how much free space we had left and would delete unneeded content from time to time, especially TV shows and movies that we'd already viewed as they took up a lot of space. We noticed that the notebook had the best Wi-Fi receiver of our devices, and in some locations, it would be the only device that was capable of accessing the Wi-Fi. Upon our return, we picked up an eleven-inch MacBook Air so that we would each have a notebook to work with. In hindsight, we could have easily gotten away with just bringing this smaller and lighter model on our trip.

We each had an iPad Mini as our tablet. We often used them as eReaders. Elizabeth's original eReader was a Kindle, which she loved until she accidentally left it in the seatback compartment on a plane, never to see it again. Fortunately, the iPad had a Kindle app that worked just fine, and we were able to share the same account, which is nice when we wanted to read the same book. The same holds true for the iBooks app where we can share books through iTunes (it just takes a little more effort to do so). We also used: Zinio to purchase and read digital magazines, Skype to make calls, Google Maps for directions, Simply Noise for white noise to help us sleep at night, AccuWeather for weather forecasts (we liked the iPhone version better than the iPad), XE for currency exchange rates, and Mail to check our email. When it came to web browsing, we relied on either Safari, Apple's default browser, or Chrome from Google, which was especially handy when we were in need of foreign language translation.

We each started out with an iPhone and describe later why we downsized to just a single phone shared between us. We used the phone's camera function on a daily basis until we picked up a digital camera a few months into the trip. We began using the preloaded camera app and then upgraded with a purchase of CP Pro, which served us a little better. Other apps that came in handy were: Clock to serve as our alarm clock; Wallet to hold our mobile boarding passes when they were available; Reminders to remind us of things that we needed to do, such as check-in for our flights; Notes to jot down our thoughts for the blog; AroundMe to see what's located in the area; Compass to help us find our way; 8 Tracks for music; WhatsApp, and Facebook. Most of the iPad applications above also appeared on our phones. We added some international airline applications as well. EasyJet, for one, had a great mobile app that made it easy to manage our bookings, check in online, and obtain mobile boarding passes.

We each brought along an iPod nano, which we primarily used when we worked out. Their small size made them ideal travel companions. We'd had them for a few years, and Rich's failed just over halfway through the trip. Since, the iPod is synched with content stored on the notebook in iTunes, he just moved the content to his iPhone and used that as a backup for the rest of the trip. When it comes to earbuds, we each brought along an extra pair of our preferred style and they got us through the trip.

When we bought our Panasonic digital camera that we cover later under *Preserving Memories*, we also purchased a 32GB SD card. This provided plenty of space for the camera to store our images and video on. Our notebook had an SD slot making it fairly easy to upload our content each day. As long as we remembered to "eject" the device before removing it, iPhoto would remember what we previously uploaded and pick up where we left off. Whenever we'd forget, it would get a little messy, but we never lost any content. Every couple of months, we would delete content on the SD card that was more than a month old. This ensured that we'd never run out of space. You can avoid this by getting a Wi-Fi-enabled camera. However, we found they cost an extra $100 and it wasn't worth that much to us.

With all your devices, you're going to need to keep them powered, and electrical outlets come in all sorts of shapes and sizes around the world. Years ago, our friend Ann from Australia turned us on to a universal power adapter that costs about $35, and we picked one up for each of us. They served us well during all of our international travels leading up to our trip and continued to perform well all over the world, except for South Africa, where we had to buy an adapter for our adapter. One of our power adapters started working inconsistently in Europe, so we ditched it and found that we could get along fine with just one. The reason for this is that all of our devices, except for our notebook, could be recharged via USB (universal serial bus) and our notebook had two USB ports. Thus, when our notebook was connected to a power source, we could rotate the charging of our mobile devices and camera via the USB ports. It would have been nice if all of our USB devices could have been charged using the same cord, but that was not case. Our Apple devices required two different USB cords, and we each carried a pair of them in our backpacks so that we had a backup. Our camera required a third type of USB cord that we somehow lost shortly after getting the camera. We searched for a long time in South America before finally finding a compatible USB power cord that was reasonably priced. We also brought along a USB adapter for the car that plugs into a car's cigarette lighter. This little adapter was invaluable to us, since our mobile phone's battery often ran low without power when we were using it to navigate on a long drive. Plugging it in and letting the car recharge the phone as we drove eliminated this problem.

Since you're probably not going to be bringing along a printer or scanner, we recommend using your phone or camera to replace the scan and copy functions, and take pictures of receipts, business cards, and similar materials that you want to retain. As for printing, you can utilize the print to PDF format and just save the digital images. If you're using compatible technology, you can then access them from any device.

The only things that we really ever needed to print were boarding passes, train tickets, and tickets for tours that we booked. We only printed these items when we knew that a digital image was not accepted. One low-cost airline we flew a few times required passengers to print their own boarding passes or face a steep fee to obtain them at the airport. So, we always made sure, in these cases, to use the free printing available at our hotel's business center. Thus, we never incurred any charges for printing during the trip. Sometimes, we could email whatever it was to the front desk to be printed for us. Other times, we used a public PC connected to a printer in a hostel or hotel business center. When doing this, we were concerned about our privacy being compromised on a public device. We always made sure that we unchecked the box that asked us if we wanted to stay logged in to Gmail. We also wiped out the browser history if we could, as some systems were more open than others. Perhaps, we were being overly paranoid, but we wanted to minimize our risk of falling victim to identity theft.

In order to preserve all your content while travelling, we recommend investing in a backup service. We subscribed to a cloud-based backup service named BackBlaze that cost us just $5 per month. Whenever we were connected to the Internet, BackBlaze would automatically go to work in the background to ensure that all of our content was backed up. This was a small price to pay for the peace of mind that, in the event that our notebook was lost, stolen, or damaged, we'd be able to recover its contents. BackBlaze also provided a cool mobile app that gave us the ability to access the backup content as long as we had an Internet connection. We took advantage of this more than once to look up information when we were away from our lodging where we usually left our notebook.

Another backup resource we used was iCloud to store copies of all of our photos and videos. Once we activated this free service (up to a 5GB limit each that we never exceeded) from Apple, the backups were taken automatically from iPhoto where we would upload the new content from our camera on a daily basis. This gave us a dual backup of content, as both BackBlaze and iCloud were backing it up. It's worth noting that this was the main reason that we learned to avoid connecting our notebook to our mobile phone's hotspot, as these backups were data intensive and would consume all of our mobile data if we weren't careful. We also backed up our iPads to iCloud, which also occurred automatically in the background when we were connected to Wi-Fi. We backed up our iPhone to Rich's notebook, and this was also enabled to automatically take place via Wi-Fi. Fortunately, we never needed to restore any of these devices, but we felt better knowing that we had a safety net just in case.

As a further safety measure, we stored copies of some of our critical documents (e.g., digital images of our passports) in Dropbox. This is a free service (up to a 2 GB limit that we never exceeded) that provides access to documents in your account from any Internet-enabled device. One could argue that we were taking some risk by storing sensitive documents in the cloud. And, it's true, we were. However, we felt that the risk of being stranded in a foreign country without any of our critical documents because they had been lost or stolen outweighed the risk of exposure that we took by storing these documents in the cloud. Once again, it actually gave us peace of mind knowing that we had backups of all of our critical documents in Dropbox.

We covered a lot of ground here. We summarize this in the *Key Ingredients* section below to help you make your own choices. We also expand upon this subject under the *Keeping in Touch* section later in the book where we cover options for connecting your devices for voice, text and data services.

Before you decide what clothing to take, you might want to decide what kind of luggage to use. We prefer not to check luggage for several reasons. First, we hate waiting for checked luggage to come out on the conveyor belts in the baggage claim areas; this can frequently take as long as half an hour or more after the plane arrives. Second, we've each had valuable items stolen from our checked bags in the past. And third, we've each had luggage lost in transit, and that's no fun at all. We were used to traveling with carry-on roller bags within the USA and on flights to Europe, but we realized from experience that the carry-on baggage dimensions for airline travel within Europe are much smaller than that for the USA. We reviewed international carry-on baggage restrictions and came to the realization that we'd need to travel light if we wanted to avoid checking our bags around the world. That's when Elizabeth started working on Rich to abandon wheeled luggage and go with backpacks. Rich was skeptical, but Elizabeth was persistent and she eventually won him over.

So, we purchased his (M/L – 2 pounds, 12 ounces) and hers (S/M – 2 pounds, 10 ounces) Osprey Farpoint 40 backpacks that would meet all known international carry-on luggage restrictions, and sure enough, they did. We also purchased Airporter LZ Travel Covers for them. We only used the travel covers a few times when it was raining, but they really proved to be worth their while as they kept everything dry inside. We came to love our backpacks and highly recommend them.

To keep our backpacks somewhat organized, we found Eagle Creek's Pack-It™ organizing systems to be invaluable. See www.eaglecreek.com/travel-system for more details. We also purchased one medium-sized air compression bag each to efficiently store our jackets. We usually didn't need jackets, and this saved space in our backpacks. We'd usually squeeze in a couple of additional items that we wore infrequently into these bags as well to conserve space.

We acquired daypacks that we could use for incidentals such as food and water that worked well throughout the trip. Rich went with a Patagonia Lightweight Travel Pack (11.4 ounces), and Elizabeth chose a Patagonia Lightweight Travel Sling (5.8 ounces). We were both happy with our choices.

We brought along a small first aid kit that we kept in Rich's daypack. We only had to use it a couple of times for ourselves, but we put it to good use when a motorcyclist dumped his bike rounding a rain-soaked curve in front of us in Siena, Italy. We were able to administer the most basic of first aid, and it was enough for him to get back on his bike and on his way again.

Clothing

You should put considerable thought into what clothing you will bring, since you probably won't have a lot of space. This will make for some difficult choices. Think about what climates you will be in, how often you will be able to (hand) wash clothes, what is comfortable, and what will blend in well with various cultures. That's right, some cultures are very conservative, and, in such locations, it's best to dress accordingly. Shoes can be the heaviest items, so take care when selecting which shoes and how many pairs you will bring. Fortunately, many companies are making more "lightweight" versions of shoes these days. So, keep an eye out for them.

We learned about the types of clothes that other world travelers and backpackers wore, and for the most part, we bought specialized clothing that was designed for this purpose. We have included a detailed list in Appendix C. Overall, the clothing choices we made served us well and lent themselves to hand-washing in sinks, bathtubs, and showers, which is something that we became quite proficient at. If you look at our travel blog, you'll probably notice that we're often wearing the same clothes, which is certainly amusing for us to see. We found the one downside to packing light was that we lacked dress clothes, and we did get turned away from a few places for being underdressed.

Purging

What do you do with your stuff while you're gone? The amount of purging you do will depend on your plans for after your trip. Do you own a home that you plan to return to? Are you renting a place and open to relocating? As we previously shared, we purged most of the possessions we had accumulated in our one-bedroom apartment.

We started out by offering the big items, such as furniture, to our family who lived in the New York/New Jersey area. We also gave a number of items away to friends. We used eBay and Craigslist to sell some items, especially things that held some value but none of our friends or family were interested in. Selling items on Craigslist or eBay may help you recoup some of the value and provide you with more money for your kitty for the trip. We passed down our car to Rich's nephew, who would be starting college in the fall. Rich had received a hand-me-down car from his great-aunt when he entered college, and it felt good to be able to pass on the tradition.

Despite all of these efforts, we still had a lot of stuff to get rid of. We stored some fine wine and tubs of keepsakes with Rich's brother, Dave. Everything else was donated to Goodwill and the Salvation Army.

We spent our last few days in an empty apartment sitting on a pair of portable folding chairs and sleeping on an air mattress on the floor.

Looking Forward

We decided before we left that we wanted to document our travels in a blog. If that's something that appeals to you and your partner, it's best to set it up before you leave so that you're all ready to start blogging when your trip begins. We actually started blogging about our preparations before we left to get ourselves familiar with the process. We provide additional information about our approach to blogging later in the book in the "Preserving Memories" section.

We anticipated meeting people on the road and decided that it would be helpful to have some business cards printed with our names, email addresses, and travel blog on them. We didn't push them on people as a form of self-promotion. Rather, when we really engaged with someone who expressed a genuine interest in our travels, we would offer them one of our cards. You may want to do the same.

The Final Details

Now, here are some important things to keep in mind when wrapping up the final details before you depart:

- Make arrangements to say goodbye to family and friends.
- If you have any company equipment, make sure it is returned.
- Place any significant valuables (e.g., wedding rings) in a safe deposit box and replace them with inexpensive ones.
- Set up postal mail forwarding to a family member or friend who doesn't mind collecting the important stuff that gets

mailed to you. They can then scan anything critical to a PDF and email it to you while you're away.

- Contact credit and debit card companies to notify them that you'll be traveling abroad for a year. That way your cards won't be denied when you try to use them in a foreign country.
- Unlock your mobile phones so you can use them with international SIM cards or buy cheap unlocked phones for the trip.
- Make arrangements for your last day or two before you leave, such as scheduling an inspection with your landlord so that you can get your security deposit back if you are moving out of a rented apartment.

Don't worry, we provide a detailed checklist of all the little final details that need to be taken care of in Appendix D.

Key Ingredients

Preparing:

Visas:

- Obtain passports if you don't have them already. If you do, make sure that they'll be valid for at least six months longer than the time you plan to be abroad and that you have sufficient blank pages for immigration stamps to be applied.
- Research visa requirements for the countries that you'd like to visit.

Immunizations:

- Use the Centers for Disease Control and Prevention's excellent health and safety information website (www.cdc.gov/travel/) to learn about immunizations and determine if any will be required.

- Determine if you'll need a prescription for anti-malaria medication and obtain one if you do.
- Consider getting a prescription for an antibiotic to treat traveler's diarrhea. (We cover this subject later in the book under "Eating Out.")

Health Insurance:

- Look into travelers' health insurance plans, select one, and obtain coverage.

Technology:

- Notebook/Tablet/Mobile Phone/Music Player/Ear Buds: decide whether you want to take none, one or two.
- Backup Service: you should consider signing up for a cloud backup service that will backup your notebook over Wi-Fi as well as backup your photos and digital documents.
- Digital Camera: the cameras on mobile phones have come a long way but digital cameras can be even better. Decide if you want to bring one. You may want to add a storage card to provide additional capacity.
- Universal Power Adapter: This device is invaluable. Decide whether you want to take one or two.
- Power and USB Cords: Make sure that you have at least one to power/recharge each of your devices.
- Printing/Scanning: You can use your mobile phone or tablet to take pictures of paper images that you want to save (such as receipts). You can also print things in PDF format and save them to one or more of your devices. When you must have a paper copy of a document, you can usually use the services offered at your lodging.
- Review the Keeping in Touch section to learn more about options for connecting your devices to voice, text and data.

Luggage:

- Decide what type of luggage you'll take and keep in mind the size and airline overhead size requirements.

Clothing:

- Decide what clothing you'll take. See our choices in Appendix C.

Purging:

- Decide what you'll do with all of your belongings while you're away.

Looking Forward:

- Decide if you're going to chronicle your adventures in a blog.
- Have business cards made up to share with fellow travelers if that idea appeals to you.

The Final Details:

- Refer to the section above to get things in order before you depart.

Pre-Arrival

Doing some basic homework before you and your partner arrive in a country can go a long way toward enhancing your experience. Of course, there are the obvious questions to be answered: How are we going to get there? Where are we going to stay? And, what are we going to do when we get there? Beyond that, however, there are many more important questions to be answered.

The first thing that we would do before arriving in a new country is some scouting to gather *essential information* that is important to know such as: Is a visa required? What's the primary language? What's the currency and exchange rate? How safe is it? Can we drink the tap water? What's the availability of ATMs? Are credit cards widely accepted? Is there any risk of malaria? We used the Internet to gather this information from various websites and created a spreadsheet to capture it.

With regard to the obvious questions, we dedicate a chapter each to the topics of transportation, lodging, and sightseeing. In response to the question, What are we going to do when we get there?, Elizabeth took advantage of her mother's public library account to borrow digital copies of various travel guides from Fodor's and Lonely Planet, which she downloaded to her tablet using the Kindle app. This was a great way to pick up some information on the places that we were visiting while saving some money. Had we thought of this before we left, we probably could have made a similar arrangement with our local library. Look into what digital lending options your local public library offers before you depart and take advantage of their offerings. You can also download information about the countries and cities that you plan to visit from websites such as Wikitravel and save them to PDF files on your tablet and/or notebook. If you don't have time to review the information before you depart, you can then read it in transit to your destination. This will give you a better sense of the local culture, food, neighborhoods, and more. You can also download phrasebooks from Wikitravel for free that can help you get a sense for the local languages.

Tip: We suggest a "divide and conquer" approach to pre-arrival planning. We suggest one of you tackles the travel and sightseeing logistics, while the other explores the essential information and prepares a scouting report.

How to Prepare Your Scouting Report

We prepared a scouting matrix to keep track of the information that we documented for each country. Here is the information that we tried to capture for each country and the resources that we used. We provide a summary of the data you'll want to consider capturing in Appendix A.

Visa Requirements

Most countries don't require special visas for US citizens, but some do and it can take a few weeks to acquire them. We always started with the US State Department's invaluable website: www.travel.state. gov. Just enter the country that you're interested in and a plethora of information is presented to you. It's an excellent resource for figuring out what the visa requirements are, if any. More importantly, it provides travel warnings, alerts, and safety and security information. We actually made decisions not to visit countries that we originally wanted to visit based on this information. We'll cover that in more detail later on in the section on "Staying Safe."

Occasionally, you may want to use the link provided to visit the website for the desired country's embassy where you can obtain additional visa information. Don't wait until the last minute to obtain your visas; you can run into issues, as we did, that can delay the process. Foreign governments prepare the forms that need to be filled out, and they often are not as clear and user friendly as you would expect. For example, on our India visa applications, there were some free-form address boxes and we failed to provide a zip code in one of them. Consequently, our applications were rejected, and we had to go through the tedious process of preparing the applications from scratch once again and resubmitting them. Needless to say, this was an exasperating experience, but there was nothing that we could do about it. So, please leave yourselves some extra time when applying for your visas.

Airport Transportation

If you have pre-booked a place to stay, you can use the Internet to figure out a cost-effective way to get from your point of entry, usually an airport, to your lodging. Start out by checking the website for your accommodation to see if they provide transportation options and directions. Next, visit the airport's website that you're flying into to see what transportation options are available. Wikitravel (www.wikitravel.org) can also be a fairly reliable resource for airport transportation options. Just enter the name of the city that you're fly-ing into and the information presented will normally include airport transportation options. Keep in mind that Wikitravel's informa-tion can be a little outdated and the transportation costs may have increased. When you're traveling by another mode of transportation, such as a train, to enter a country, you can find this information by visiting the train station's website. If you haven't pre-booked your lodging, you may want to use a similar approach to figure out trans-portation that will get you to an area where you can plan to begin your quest for lodging.

Currency

A simple Google search using "currency" and the name of the coun-try is the quickest way to learn about a country's form of money. You will also often learn about a country's currency when review-ing a website like Wikitravel. Regardless, once you know what the currency is, we suggest using www.xe.com to look up the current exchange rate and make note of it in your matrix. This site makes it easy to see how the exchange rate is trending over time. We found this helpful to get a sense of whether a country was becoming more or less expensive to visit. We also suggest installing XE's app on your mobile phone and/or tablet. Once you pre-load a currency in the app, it will still work when the device is offline, which we found useful.

ATM Availability

ATMs can be scarce in some countries, and fees can vary widely. Try using the websites for both Lonely Planet and Fodor's Travel for this topic. On www.lonelyplanet.com, enter the country you're interested in and then select the entry for the country when the results are returned. Next, select the tab for "In Detail" and then select "Money & costs" under the heading of "Planning tools." Here you'll often find a subsection on "ATMs." On www.fodors.com, enter the country you're interested in and then select the entry for the country. Next, select the tab for "TRAVEL TIPS" and then select "Money" under the heading of "CONTACTS & RESOURCES." Here you'll often find a subsection on "ATMS AND BANKS."

Credit Card Acceptance

Once again, the websites for both Lonely Planet and Fodor's Travel provide good insight. On www.lonelyplanet.com, enter the country you're interested in and then select the entry for the country when the results are returned. Next, select the tab for "In Detail" and then select "Money & Costs" under the heading of "Planning tools." Here you'll often find a subsection on "Credit Cards." On www.fodors.com, enter the country you're interested in and then select the entry for the country. Next, select the tab for "TRAVEL TIPS" and then select "Money" under the heading of "CONTACTS & RESOURCES." Look for a subsection on "CREDIT CARDS."

Language

A simple Google search using "official language of" and the name of the country is the quickest way to learn about the languages spoken in a country. One of the top results returned will be a link to Wikipedia. We would often drill down on this site to learn more. The primary language spoken in a country can vary, so it's important to dig deeper than just the official language of a country. Switzerland is a good example. There, French dominates in the south, while German is dominant in the north. Once you know the primary language, you may want to learn more about the language. We cover this subject in more depth in the "Language Barriers" section.

Time Zone

Use the World Clock website at www.timeanddate.com/worldclock/ and enter the name of the largest city nearest your destination. This website has a great interactive time zone map that makes it easy to see the differences in time zones. You can log the offset to GMT (Greenwich Mean Time) and use this to gain a relative comparison to the time zone that you'll be coming from as well as the time back home, which for us was GMT-4.

Can We Drink the Water?

We had a great website dedicated to answering the question, "Can I drink the water?" but alas, toward the tail end of our trip, the site went out of business. No matter, we always tried to double-check our findings with other websites. Once again, a simple Google search using "can I drink the water in" and the name of the country is the quickest way to learn about the safety of a country's tap water. You can then use the websites for both Lonely Planet and Fodor's Travel to verify your findings. You just need to work a little harder to find the answers. On www.lonelyplanet.com, enter the country you're interested in and then select the entry for the country when the results are returned. Next, select the tab for "NEED TO KNOW" and then select "Health & Safety" under the heading of "Practical Information." Here you'll often find a subsection on "Water." On www.fodors.com, enter the country you're interested in and then select the entry for the country.

Next, select the tab for "TRAVEL TIPS" and then select "Health" under the heading of "CONTACTS & RESOURCES."

Local Sim Card

Obtaining a local SIM card in the country you're visiting can be useful to get a cheaper data and calling plan for the time you'll be there. This is especially helpful if your Wi-Fi is spotty and you can use the SIM card as a hotspot or just to look up information on the web from your phone. Identifying the top two or three mobile carriers in a country is a good starting point. You can then look for one of them upon your arrival to see what options they offer. Begin with a Google search using "top mobile carriers in" along with the name of the country and then drill down from there until you're able to identify the top carriers.

Tipping Guidelines

When it comes to tipping, recommendations vary from resource to resource. So, it's advisable to check a few different sites to get a sense of how much to tip for services at restaurants, taxis, hairstylists, and the like. Check to see what Wikitravel, Lonely Planet, and/or Fodor's have to say.

Crime Advisories

Start with the US State Department's website as described under "Visas" in this chapter and review the "Safety and Security" tab for the country you're interested in. Then consult Wikitravel and Fodor's as well. Wikitravel usually has a section labeled "Stay Safe." On the Fodor's website, review the "Safety" section under the heading of "CONTACTS & RESOURCES."

Disease/Malaria Risks

As previously mentioned under the "Immunizations/Prescriptions" section, we suggest using the Centers for Disease Control and Prevention's website (www.cdc.gov/travel/) to learn about malaria risks. On the CDC's website, search for the "Vaccines and Medicines" section for each country you plan to visit and pay special attention to the subsection for "Malaria" to determine if you should take the preventative medication on your trip. You may need to start the medication in advance of your arrival. So, be sure to review the instructions for whatever medication you've decided to bring and be sure that you clearly understand when to start the medication, how frequently it should be taken, and if you need to continue taking it after you leave the country where you face the risk, as we did with Malarone.

Common Scams

The reality of being a traveler in a foreign country is that you become a target for various con artists. Learning about common scams that are being perpetrated on local tourists heightens your awareness and helps to reduce your risk of falling prey to such antics. Wikitravel and the US State Department's website are two good resources for learning about scams. For a good example, just take a look at the Wikitravel entry for Bangkok, where you'll find an entire section dedicated to "Scams."

Departure Tax/Fee

No one likes to arrive at the airport for a departure to learn that, before you can even check in for your flight, you first need to pay a departure tax in cash to the local government. Departure taxes are common, but they're usually embedded in the cost of the airline ticket so you're not even aware that you're paying one. However, we encountered departure taxes in a few countries such as Bali that were not included in the airfare. Searching for "Departure Tax" on Wikipedia is a good place to start to see if a departure tax has to be paid. Be sure to check out what forms of payment are accepted as some governments only accept cash. Departure taxes aren't just limited to international flights. You may also encounter them when flying within a country as we did in Argentina when we flew from Ushuaia to Buenos Aires. So, it's also a good practice to check the local airport's website to avoid any surprises.

Notes

It's always helpful to have a catchall category in your scouting report to make a note of something important that you discover about a country. As an example, for Argentina, we made a note to only use radio taxis that you call, taxis from a stand, or a "remise" (private car and driver). Of course, the one time that we chose to ignore this note, we ran into a problem (see the "Staying Safe" section). Feel free to modify the scouting data captured and resources used to fit your needs. For instance, we didn't include an entry for weather, but you may want to. Checking the weather was something that we just always did without thinking. In fact, at times, Rich would become obsessive about it. The primary driver for our return visit to New Zealand was to see the fjords at the world renowned Milford Sound, which is known as the wettest inhabited place in New Zealand. We chose not to visit the fjords during our first trip to New Zealand and regretted our omission ever since we saw how magnificent Norway's fjords were. Thus, Rich kept checking the AccuWeather app's long-range forecast in advance of our arrival in New Zealand to try to figure out which day would be best to visit Milford Sound. We planned to adjust the schedule for our seven-day trip to New Zealand around the optimum time to visit Milford Sound. Rich's pre-arrival obsession paid off; we were rewarded with a gorgeous day to take in the spectacular sights. While there's no doubt that luck also plays a role when it comes to weather, prearrival planning can be rewarding and is often worth the effort.

Key Ingredients

Pre-Arrival:

- Prepare a scouting report for, at least, your first few destinations on visas, airport transportation, currency, ATM availability, credit cards, time zones, water, SIM cards, crime, disease, scams, taxes, and anything else you feel relevant. See our guide in Appendix A.

Main Course

Living the Dream

Getting From Point A to Point B

Transportation

Figuring out your transportation can certainly keep you busy during your trip. Depending upon costs and availability, you may find yourselves in a place you didn't originally plan to visit because you happened upon a great airfare or train deal. Sometimes you can get great last-minute deals, but more often you will need to book tickets at least two weeks in advance of your departure date to obtain reasonable airfares. We tried to be as flexible as possible so that we could stay in a place longer if we were really enjoying ourselves or leave a place sooner if we weren't comfortable. In this chapter, we break down long-distance transportation into the main types you might use: planes, trains, buses, and ferries/boats followed by local transportation including car rentals, metros, trams, buses, and taxis as a last resort.

Before we cover the various modes of transportation, and share our experiences with each, it's worth noting that it's helpful to get in the habit of logging your itineraries where they're easy to find. You never know when you're going to need to check on the departure and/or arrival time or reference the confirmation number. Printing each itinerary was impractical. So, we got into the habit of creating a PDF of the itinerary and transferring it to the iBooks application on one of our tablets and/or our mobile phone. That way, we always had fairly easy access to it.

Plane

Given a choice of transportation for long-distance travel, we prefer flying mainly because it's the quickest. This enables you to spend more time sightseeing and less time in transit. That said, air travel can be quite expensive, making other forms of transportation more attractive for those of us on a budget.

Your desire to be spontaneous and make last-minute decisions on where to go next might get compromised as airfare prices often spike the closer you get to your departure date. This forced us to start planning further ahead than we wanted to. If we didn't, then our travel costs would start spiraling out of control. Thus, we had to start booking our air travel two weeks in advance or more. Consequently, we weren't able to extend our stays in some of the locations we liked best, and it caused us to forfeit several airfares because of an unforeseen circumstance that we'll tell you about later in the book. Our advice to you is to keep an eye on airfares and to be prepared to book a few weeks in advance so that you aren't faced with escalating costs.

There are countless different airlines around the world. The good news is that you can find well-run budget airlines, which provide safe, affordable travel, all over the world. One thing that really helped us was that we were traveling with backpacks that met the carry-on requirements of every airline we flew. If we'd had to check luggage, our costs would have gone up dramatically because the budget airlines charge high fees to check bags.

A great tool that can help you decide where to go next is

www.skyscanner.com. This site has a nifty tool where you can enter your current location and type in "Everywhere" as the destination. It pulls in all the locations you can fly to along with the costs. Here's an example of how we used this in Italy: We knew that we were going to finish up in Sicily, where there are two primary airports: Catania and Palermo. So, we ran searches from each airport to "Everywhere." We discovered an unbelievable airfare to Marseille, France. This destination wasn't on our original list, but we did want to get to France and we'd never been to Marseille. So, we jumped on it, booked the flight, and then found an equally amazing deal on a Holiday Inn Express near the airport. It turns out that we loved Marseille and hope to return there again someday.

You can also use this tool in reverse if you know where you want to go and you want to find the cheapest places to get there from. Say you really want to go to Taiwan while you're in Asia but want to find out the cheapest places from which to get there. You can enter "Taiwan" in the *From* field and "Everywhere" in the *To* field, and you'll find that there are numerous places within Asia where you can fly from Taiwan to for under $100. Now, you can pick some of these places and try entering them in the *From* field and enter "Taiwan" in the *To* field and you'll usually find similarly attractive airfares. By playing around with this tool, we uncovered numerous airfare deals that we took advantage of.

If you know the two points you want to fly between but are flexible on the date, then we recommend using matrix.itasoftware. com's "see calendar of lowest fares" search option. This highlights in orange the departure day or days when the fare is the lowest. Once you click on the price, it brings up a list of the airlines offering that fare along with travel times and stops (if any).

If you're not finding a good fare using the primary tools we recommend, then try some other tools to see what fares are available. Much to our surprise, some websites have deals that others don't. We ended up booking flights on Orbitz when we found lower cost fares there that didn't show up on the other sites that we searched.

Rather than pay to fly, why not use points for free travel? We were fortunate to have accumulated a lot of frequent flier miles. They saved us a lot of money and offered us tremendous flexibility because we could usually modify our bookings without incurring any change fees. To make the most of your points, we recommend reserving them for long hauls and the highest fares so that you can save the most money. They're also great for one-way travel because the airlines usually don't gouge you for a one-way fare using points like they often do for a cash fare. A good value use of points with United Airlines is to take advantage of its "Saver Awards." These fares can be as low as 10,000 points one way. The best way to find them is to select the options "My Dates are Flexible" and search by "Award Travel" right from United's home page along with your *From* and *To* airports. Once you click the Search button, you'll be presented with a colorful calendar showing the dates offering Saver Awards. Just click on one of the color-coded dates to see what flight options and point costs are available to you. Once you play around with this tool for a while, you will start to see its potential. Playing around like this is how we discovered the Saver Award deal that took us from Hawaii to Peru in first class for just 45,000 miles each.

Sometimes you also need to use some ingenuity to get from where you are to where you want to be. You may have a loose plan for travelling nonstop from one destination to another, but what happens when there are no affordable flights between those places?

We ran into this problem when we started looking for ways to get from New Zealand to South America. Looking at the map, we thought surely there would be direct flights between these two parts of the world. And there were but the prices were outrageous – well over $1,000 apiece for a one-way fare. We were reluctant to pay for such pricey airfares, so it was time to get creative.

We started searching on United Airline's website to see how we might use frequent flier miles to somehow get to South America. We couldn't find anything reasonable from New Zealand. So, we looked at flying from Australia but had no luck there either. We expanded our search to other Pacific destinations that we wouldn't mind visiting on our way to South America. Lo and behold, we found a sweet deal from Honolulu to Lima, Peru, for just 25,000 miles each in coach or 45,000 miles in first class. We had the miles, so we decided to splurge and go first class since we'd be traveling for more than twenty-four hours to get there. It would require us to travel on Thanksgiving Day, making stops in Salt Lake City, Utah, and Houston, Texas. We hadn't planned on returning to the USA during our trip, but having met in Hawaii and subsequently honey-mooning there, we've always had a soft spot for the islands. Given Hawaii's natural beauty, it wouldn't be the end of the world if we had to stop over there during our trip.

Before booking the trip, we had to check for reasonable one-way airfares from New Zealand to Hawaii. Unfortunately, there were no "cheap" fares to be found, but we were able to find fares on Air New Zealand that when added together were still well below the cost of a single one-way ticket from New Zealand to South America. So, we rationalized the fares as the best that we could find and part of the price that we had to pay to get to South

America. We even worked it out so that we would be able to spend a few enjoyable days in Hawaii.

Here's another example of how we put frequent flyer miles to good use. We found that flying within South America was expensive, especially within Argentina, where the lower fares are reserved for Argentinean citizens and tourists are forced to pay significantly higher airfares. We wanted to fly from Buenos Aires to Ushuaia at the southern tip of South America, then to El Calafate in the heart of Patagonia and back to Buenos Aires. The airfare for each of us for this multicity trip was more than $800 on Aerolíneas Argentina, which happens to be part of the SkyTeam Airline Alliance. There isn't a lot of competition in the Argentinean market. Thus, this was the best fare that we could find.

Delta Airlines is part of SkyTeam. Rich had about 22,000 miles banked in his Delta account. So, we looked up the cost of reward travel using Delta miles and discovered that we could book this trip for 16,000 miles each. On average, an airline mile is worth about one penny. So, 16,000 miles is normally worth about $160 in air travel. In this case, however, we had the chance to get an $800 airfare for only 16,000 miles. This was an incredible deal. After researching further, we found that we could transfer Starwood Hotel points one-for-one to our Delta account. We still had quite a few Starwood points, so we transferred 10,000 Starwood points into our Delta account, and we were able to book both of us on the itinerary that we wanted. We were thrilled to save ourselves $1,600.

One more airline travel tool worth mentioning is www. seatguru.com. Where you sit on a plane, especially on long-distance flights, can make a huge difference on how you experience a flight. Seatguru not only helps you identify the best seats on the plane, such as those with extra leg room, but it also helps you avoid the worst seats on the plane, such as those that don't recline. We always made a point to look up our flights on Seatguru in advance to try to select the best seats possible. For example, we learned when flying on a 747, there were a few sets of dual seats toward the back of the planes that we dubbed poor-man's first class. We reserved them whenever we could. You should, too.

Train

When air travel doesn't make sense, our recommendation would be to travel by train. They're usually comfortable and reliably on time. The biggest obstacle we found with train travel is that many train travel websites are not very user friendly; are not offered in English; and will not allow you to purchase tickets online. One company, RailEurope, is capitalizing on this, taking information from local train operators and offering a platform that is easy to use in English where you can buy tickets throughout Europe. However, RailEurope tacks on high fees for this service. With just a little extra digging and a few stops at the local train depots, you can save a lot of money and avoid the RailEurope fees.

For researching and booking train travel, we recommend www.seat61.com. We used it frequently. Train travel can be really handy when you're moving about within one country and do not want to rent a car. Many countries have good train systems that can connect you to just about anywhere, often when you can't get there on an airplane.

We used trains here and there throughout the trip. Our first experience, though, was the most exasperating. We were on the first leg of our trip in Beijing, China, and wanted to visit Xi'an, a city made famous for its army of ancient terracotta warriors. Xi'an was about six hundred miles away from Beijing. Airfares were expensive, while train fares seemed reasonable. Basically, we found two choices online: high-speed trains that get you there in about five hours or sleeper trains that get you there overnight in about twelve hours. We decided to go with the high-speed train and found a time with availability that suited us.

Our troubles started when we couldn't book tickets online less than four days out and we needed to leave in three days. We'd read that the train station in Beijing can be a madhouse. So, just to be safe, we decided to pay a visit the day before our trip to buy our tickets and familiarize ourselves with the station. When we arrived, we found a few self-serve kiosks, but they only took Chinese citizen credit cards. We next tried the ticket windows, where after waiting in line for about twenty minutes we were then instructed that we needed to get into a different and much longer line that was the "English" line. When we finally made our way up to the attendant we found out we had to pay in cash. Now we had to find an ATM. The ones nearby either weren't working or we couldn't get them to recognize our PIN. Over an hour had passed at this point and it was starting to get dark out. We didn't want to leave without getting our train tickets, so we left the station in pursuit of an ATM that would work. Elizabeth finally found one that accepted our PIN, so we completed the transaction, took the cash and headed back to the station.

Now, back at the train station and in the English line, we got into an even longer queue than before and endured a long staff shift change. Finally, we repeated the process of ordering our tickets and fortunately they're still available. We hand the clerk our cash, but wait, there's one final hurdle. She needs to see our passports. We didn't know that we needed them to buy train tickets for travel within the country. Fortunately, we were staying in a hostel without a safe and Rich chose to keep the passports on him in a zippered pocket rather than lock them up in his backpack. More than two hours after we'd arrived at the Beijing train station, we were somewhat frazzled, but we had our train tickets at last. Woo-hoo! It was a good thing that we came a day early or else we would have missed our train.

Our lesson learned was not to wait until the last minute to book train fares in countries where English is not the primary language. Its also helpful to utilize various travel forums, to gain insight into the local train travel options and ticket purchasing process.

Another country where we took advantage of train travel was in Japan. We'd read good things about Japan's rail system, and while expensive, we decided to purchase a fourteen-day rail pass that would give us the freedom to move around the country at will. One thing to know ahead of time is that the pass cannot be purchased within Japan. Thus, we had to pay for the pass in advance and have it shipped to a hotel that we knew that we'd be staying at in Taipei, Taiwan. In the end, Japan's rail system lived up to our expectations and then some. The trains were fast, clean, and efficient. They were consistently on time, and the high-speed Shinkansen (bullet) trains really flew while providing a smooth, comfortable ride. We used www.hyperdia.com, an invaluable companion, to easily find the combination of trains that we needed to get from place to place. We were also impressed that every train station had a tourist information center with an English-speaking attendant. We found them extremely helpful.

In Europe, our train experiences were good overall. Elizabeth discovered a deal in Italy where tickets were priced at two-for-one on Saturdays, and we twice took advantage of this deal. We also encountered a brief rail strike in Italy, but it did not affect our travel plans. We had an unpleasant train ride from Zagreb, Croatia to Budapest, Hungary. It was a five-hour trip. So, we decided to pay for first-class seats, thinking that we'd be more comfortable during the long ride. What a mistake that was. The first-class seats were nothing special, and people who paid for coach tickets filled in the mostly empty first-class seats, which we could have also done. In addition, it was a hot summer day. The train lacked air-conditioning, and most of the windows either couldn't be opened or only opened a few inches. Thus, we were basically baked on this train ride. Another lesson learned here is that we should have done a better job researching the train's ticket classes and amenities before booking the trip. It's also interesting to note that it was cheaper to buy a round-trip ticket than a one-way ticket even though we wouldn't be returning to Zagreb. How did we know this? We learned about it on www.seat61.com. Enterprising locals in Budapest who were aware of this were asking passengers like us for our return tickets. We had no use for them, and so we obliged them. The remainder of our train travel in Europe was fine, but prices in Western Europe were much higher than Eastern Europe. Then again, the quality of the trains was much better as well.

Bus

From what we could see, buses appeared to be the most economical form of long-distance travel unless, of course, you hitchhike as some backpackers do. Even though we had taken a year off to travel and had lots of time, bus travel often was too slow for us. We were just too impatient. That's why we didn't use buses more frequently.

We traveled by bus occasionally in South America, where we found it to be both comfortable and economical. The air-conditioning could have been better in the hot weather, but it was nothing like the train ride to Budapest. We chronicle our twenty-hour New Year's Eve bus ride from Salta to Mendoza, Argentina, a little later in the book under "Lodging." After our stay in Mendoza, we opted for another bus ride to take us to Santiago, Chile, over the scenic Los Libertadores Pass. This was a nine-hour trip including two and a half hours spent at the Argentina/Chile border crossing going through immigration and customs. We made this trip during the day so that we could admire the beauty of crossing the Andes. It was stunning. We also selected the bus over flying as it saved us quite a bit of money. If we had flown into Santiago, we would have had to pay expensive airfares and an additional $160 each in reciprocity fees to enter Chile. For whatever reason, these fees are not collected when you enter the country at a border crossing by land.

One word of caution about bus travel: The bus stations aren't always located in the best areas of a city, which we found out the hard way when we arrived in Santiago. The location of the terminal was in a run-down part of the city that we did not feel comfortable walking through. Fortunately, it was daytime, and we were able to take a taxi to a much nicer part of the city. If you're going to be traveling by bus, we suggest doing some research on the location of the bus stations before you plan your travel.

For local, intercity travel, if you haven't rented a car or the metro or tram won't get you to where you want to go, the bus can be a good option. We're not big fans of local buses for a couple of reasons. They're often slow and late. Thus, we lack the patience required to be regular bus riders. That said, we took our fair share of buses, and they always got us to where we wanted to go even if it took longer than we'd like.

Rental Car

In less congested cities and parts of the world, a rental car is a great option for travel. We traveled throughout Asia without ever renting a car. Then, we frequently rented cars throughout the rest of our trip. In hindsight, we should have rented a car in Phuket, Thailand, and possibly Bali. In the USA, just about all of the car rentals have automatic transmissions. It's the exact opposite in the rest of the world, where manual transmissions dominate. If you want to rent a car with an automatic transmission outside of the USA, you'll pay dearly for it. Since Rich is comfortable driving a manual transmission, he became the designated driver by default and Elizabeth took on the role of navigator.

Driving might prove to be a little more challenging in the British-influenced countries, where cars drive on the left side of the road and the driver and passenger positions are also opposite the USA norm. In such cases, the stick shift is on the left side of the driver instead of the right, which takes some getting used to. Elizabeth relied heavily on the Google Maps app to navigate us all over the world, and it came through time and time again with a few exceptions. One of the few times that it failed us was in Valparaíso, Chile, which has steep hills that make San Francisco's streets look tame. Occasionally, the app would take us up a road that turned from pavement to dirt and then dead-ended. We were able to take it in stride and got some good laughs out of it. At other times, the app would guide us down a road that looked more like an alley where it was questionable whether or not a car could fit through. On one occasion in Sicily, the street Elizabeth told Rich to take looked so narrow that he was afraid to attempt it. But then, when another car entered the alleyway and went through without getting stuck, Rich decided to try it. It was a tight fit, but we did reach our final destination. Navigating was often a full-time job. It also helped immensely to have two sets of eyes on the road; Elizabeth saved Rich from potentially dangerous situations on numerous occasions.

The cost of rental cars varies from continent to continent. We found that they were expensive in Oceania and South America, inexpensive in South Africa, and moderately priced in Europe. We booked our rental cars using a credit card that included liability insurance coverage. This enabled us to decline the insurance coverage that usually cost $15 per day or more. We were fortunate in that we didn't get into any accidents during our trip. However, we did scratch up a few bumpers along the way. The bumpers were always made of molded plastic, and when they got damaged, the scratches would show up as white against whatever color the car was. We didn't want to incur any extra fees. So, when we knowingly scratched up a bumper, we would buy a magic marker that most closely matched the color of the car and then color in the scratches. Each time we did this, it worked, and we had no issues when we returned the car. The funny thing is that there were a couple of times when we turned our car in and the attendant gave us a hard time about scratches on the car that we know we didn't cause. When this happened, we somehow always talked our way out of it, and we never encountered any additional charges.

When driving in foreign countries, it is interesting to observe how the locals drive. We were somewhat shocked in Argentina where most of the local intersections lack any signage at all, making it a free-for-all that made driving rather stressful. In Sicily, we encountered the most aggressive drivers. It was as if we were all in a race competing for every inch of space against our fellow drivers. While in South Africa, we were impressed by how courteous the drivers were. On two-lane roads (one in each direction), South African drivers would often pull over onto the shoulder, while maintaining their speed, and allow faster moving vehicles like ours to pass them. By the way, we also accumulated a few speeding tickets on our trip when we were caught by automated camera systems. The tickets were mailed to our USA mailing address with lots of threatening language if we failed to pay them. We tossed them all in the trash with no repercussions to speak of. We're not encouraging you to follow our example. We're just relaying our surprise and being honest about how we decided to handle it. Please be aware that just as in the USA, there are automated speed traps in other parts of the world.

Many of the cars we drove lacked power accessories. At home, we were accustomed to keyless entry, power locks, steering, seats, windows, side mirrors and cruise control. Most of the cars we rented had power steering, at least, and some had keyless entry. However, as luck would have it, on the day the temperatures reached into the 90s, our only choice was a car that lacked air-conditioning. Once we moved into Europe, a couple of times we got lucky and were upgraded at no extra charge to a nice car with leather seats, automatic transmission, and power everything. We thoroughly enjoyed our time in these cars.

The majority of the cars we drove took unleaded fuel, but a number of them had diesel engines and these seemed to be the most fuel-efficient. Mileage varied dramatically from model to model with some getting around twenty-five miles per gallon on the low end and up to over fifty miles per gallon on some diesel models. When given a choice, we reserved a diesel-powered car. Fuel was consistently expensive and close to double or more of what we would pay back home. In the worst case, the fuel cost over $10 a gallon at a refueling station on an autostrada in Italy.

Metro

If you have access to a metro, we recommend using that as your mode of transportation. This will often save you time and money. In many cities, we relied on their mass transportation systems. We found excellent metro systems all over the world but not necessarily in every city. The challenge always was figuring out the fare system and how to pay for the ride. Some systems make it easy—you paid a fixed fare for each use of the system regardless of your destination. Some based fares on the number of zones you passed through. Some required us to identify the starting and ending stations. Most systems had kiosks that dispensed an entry token of some kind that included: smart cards, plastic discs, metal coins, paper tabs, etc. Most kiosks accepted credit cards, but some did not, and if we only had a large bill, we ended up with a pocketful of unwanted change. Many metro stations have an attendant who can help explain these nuances, so don't feel that you need to have every metro system figured out before you arrive at your destination.

The least expensive metro systems we found were in China, and the most expensive was in Vienna, Austria. One frustrating thing about the metros in China was that everyone had to have their bags scanned and go through a metal detector. Normally, that wouldn't be a problem, except usually there was only a single line at the checkpoint. Given the number of people using the metros in China, it often took ten minutes or so just to get through security.

Surprisingly, the majority of the metro systems had signage in English (usually subtitles), and many had announcements in English that followed the native language announcements. Of course, we made a few mistakes along the way. The worst was when we underpaid the fare, and we couldn't exit the station in Kyoto, Japan. It took a while to find someone who could help us get things straightened out. All in all, we were consistently impressed with the metro systems of the world. They tended to be clean, efficient, and reasonably priced.

Tram

Quite a few cities have electric trams that run on the streets and either supplement the metro system or serve as a primary form of mass transportation in addition to buses. We liked trams because they tended to run frequently. Since they ran above ground, it was also a good way to see the local neighborhoods. On a few occasions, we rode a tram for the full circuit and back again just to see the sights. Many of the trams were on the honor system. We would buy our tickets and validate them, but usually no one ever checked them. Nevertheless, we always paid our fares just to be safe. Still, we ran into a problem in Milan.

We had taken a tram from our hotel on the outskirts of Milan into the heart of the city. As we exited the tram, Rich threw our tickets into a trashcan. Soon thereafter, we were approached by three uniformed transit officers asking to see our tickets. Not understanding them since they were speaking in Italian, we kept walking. They pursued us. Fortunately, one of them spoke some English and asked to see our tickets. They weren't satisfied with our explanation that we'd thrown them out. So, we had to go back to the trashcan and fish them out. This took a while because we weren't the only ones who threw their tickets in that particular receptacle. Since the tickets expire ninety minutes after they're validated, we had to find "our" valid tickets, which we eventually did and the officers finally let us go. Amusing now, it was not so at that moment.

Taxi/Tuk-Tuk

We recommend using taxis only as a last resort because they are expensive and the costs are often unclear. If the previous modes of transportation we list above were not available to us or it was late at night, we'd hail a taxi. We've had our share of issues with shady taxi drivers over the years. Many taxi drivers don't speak English or don't let on that they do, which makes for challenges negotiating the fare when they don't have a meter or won't use the one that they do have, which occurred more than once. To be fair, we've had some great taxi drivers over the years as well. It's just that the sour taste of the problematic drivers stays permanently etched in our minds. And, with so many lower-cost options available, it's hard to justify the added expense of a taxi.

Another type of taxi more well known throughout Asia are tuk-tuks, which are three-wheeled open-air vehicles. We have a similar view of them as we do of taxis. We used them out of convenience when our preferred methods of transportation were unavailable. We've had both good and bad experiences with tuk-tuk drivers.

Ship/Boat/Ferry

Travelling by ship, boat or ferry can be a very sensible mode of transportation, especially if flying is expensive or limited. Several cities that we visited were located on major waterways, and on occasion, we used a water taxi, hydrofoil, or ferry to transport us. We enjoyed taking them in cities like Bangkok, Thailand, and Venice, Italy. One major drawback is that weather can disrupt such travel. We found this out the hard way in Italy. We took a two-for-one train on a Saturday from Rome to Salerno. From there, we planned to take a ferry to the town of Positano, where we were staying. We walked more than half a mile with our backpacks to the ferry terminal only to find that the ferries weren't running that day due to rough seas. The water looked calm to us, but what did we know? So, we had to walk back to the train station and find alternate transportation. Fortunately, there was a bus leaving within the hour that provided a breathtaking ride along the Amalfi Coast that got us safely to our destination.

We also used a ferry ship in Scotland to transport our rental car and us from Oban to Islay. This was about a three-and-a-half-hour journey each way. It was comfortable and relaxing. The weather was decent, providing calm seas and a smooth ride most of the time. Overall, our water travels went well, and we would gladly use these modes of transportation again.

Tours

If you're looking for some guidance on what to see and do, taking a tour with a professional tour guide/tour company can take the pressure off of you trying to figure out everything on your own. We like exploring on our own, but every now and then, we signed up for a tour, and when we did, we tended to really enjoy them. We would, of course, research the tours beforehand, and as a result, we almost always had excellent guides. We found our guides to be extremely knowledgeable, not only about the sights that we were visiting, but also about local culture and customs. One of the side benefits of tours is that they can be very social, which was an unexpected benefit. We had an opportunity to interact with lots of English-speaking travelers from all around the world. This was both fun and informative, trading travel tips and recommendations with each other.

We found Viator to be a consistently reliable broker for high-quality tours around the world. It offers a great website at www.viator.com and mobile app. Viator wasn't the only tour company that we used, but we used it the most. While we welcomed the social aspect of group tours, occasionally we got lucky and were the only ones on the tour. In these cases, we received the undivided attention of the tour guide, leaving us with even greater insights. Many of the tours that we took included transportation from our hotel to our destination and back. A one-day tour in Taiwan actually included transportation on a plane, bus, and train. The ultimate, though, was our ten-day African safari where all transportation was provided enabling us to concentrate on enjoying the sights and sounds.

Hop On/Hop Off

Most major cities have hop on/hop off buses that run routes covering many of the main attractions. They're a great way to see the most popular sights in a city, and you can ride them all day and stay as long as you like at the attractions you're most interested in. We took great advantage of them in Cape Town, South Africa, and really couldn't believe what a terrific value they offered.

Hotel Shuttles

Some of the hotels where we stayed offered shuttle service to local attractions. We must admit that we did not take advantage of them very often because the shuttles run on infrequent schedules and we're not patient travelers. They're usually free. However, the drivers are often looking for a tip. So, it helps to have some local currency in small denominations with you.

Key Ingredients

Getting From Point A to Point B – Transportation:

* Log your itineraries in a place where they are easy to find.

Plane:

* Consider booking your air travel at least two weeks in advance before the fares start rising dramatically.

Train:

* When evaluating train travel, be sure to check www.seat61.com to see what this helpful site has to say before purchasing your tickets.

Bus:

* If you're on a tight budget and you've got time to spare, give this form of travel serious consideration.

Rental Car:

* You may be able to save the cost of liability insurance if you use a credit card that provides such coverage. Be sure to check the fine print because not all foreign countries are covered and you need to be comfortable with the details and paying up-front, out-of-pocket costs if your car is damaged.

Metro, Tram, and Local Bus Systems:

- Do a little research online in advance of using a transportation system. View a map and get a sense of the lines that operate and where they go. Try to also get an idea of how the fares are determined so that you're prepared.

Taxi/Tuk-Tuk:

- Do some research to understand which operators are considered safe and whether they use meters or fares are negotiated in advance.
- Find out what the local custom is on tipping.
- Learn some key phrases in the local language so that you communicate with the driver.
- Have your lodging location written down in the local language.
- Make sure that you have enough local currency to cover the fare.

Ship/Boat/Ferry:

- Travel by ship/boat/ferry is not really our thing, but some people love it. We used it strategically when it was the only cost-effective option available to us. Move it up in priority, if it's your preferred mode of transportation.
- Since weather can affect travel by water, be sure to check in advance if the boat or ferry service is in operation on the day you plan to use it.

Tours:

- Consider a tour that includes transportation from and to your hotel for a day trip as a special treat. Research reviews of the tour operator in advance on a site such as TripAdvisor or Viator.

Hop On/Hop Off:

- Read online reviews. Some cities have multiple options, so it pays to read reviews online before selecting one.

Hotel Shuttles:

- Have some local currency in small denominations in case you want to tip the driver.

Arrival Essentials

Now that you've read about your different transportation options, it's time to think about the arrival essentials so you're prepared to enter a new country. If you're entering a new country by plane, train, bus, or ship, you'll start out in an airport, station, or terminal of some sort. The first order of business is often to clear immigration. If you've done your homework on visas, you should be aware of the immigration process. The immigration lines can sometimes be severely long. So, here are a few tips intended to reduce your wait time:

- Try to get seats close to the exit if practical, and be ready to go when you arrive so that you'll be among the first passengers to disembark.
- The flight crew often distributes immigration cards before you arrive. Make sure that you carry a pen with you and fill out the immigration cards in advance of your arrival.
- If you're being bused from the plane or ship to the terminal, try to end up as close to the exit doors as possible so that you can hop off first.

While these tactics may seem trivial to you, we hate standing in line and have yet to get accustomed to it. Even though we had all the time in the world, the reality was that "travel days" were the least fun. If we could shave a few minutes off of them, especially from standing in lines, we would take some consolation in doing so.

Once you clear immigration, here are some things to seek out:

- Find an ATM.
- Buy a SIM card.
- Gather a local map and a travel brochure or two.
- Find your local transportation.
- Ok, well maybe you'll have a fifth objective, which may be the most immediate one: locate the restrooms.

You'll probably need to obtain some local currency, and ATMs are often the most cost-effective way to do this. The amount you withdraw depends upon how long you plan to be in that particular country and how widely credit cards are accepted there (be sure to research credit card acceptability before arrival). The logical thing might be to withdraw the maximum amount allowed to minimize the number of ATM withdrawals and fees that you may incur. However, the money exchangers at the airports typically offer poor exchange rates and charge high transaction fees. Thus, you want to leave the country with little or no currency left in your pockets. So, figuring out how much to withdraw upfront is part art and part science. By the end of the trip, we had mastered our money management so that we were left with little to no local currency when departing a country. Whatever we did have left, we donated to UNICEF or some other charitable organization that usually had drop boxes scattered throughout the terminal.

Finding a SIM card for your phone when you arrive can be

hit or miss. Some places have multiple carriers competing for your business. Some places offer only one choice, while others offer none at all. Part of your pre-arrival research should include identifying the top mobile carriers for the country. Then, you will have a list of preferred companies to buy from. However, when the preferred carrier is not available, consider a lesser carrier if the price is right. Ideally, purchase the SIM card and have it installed by the clerk at the counter and verify that both voice and data are working on your device, if possible. Sometimes, it takes an hour or so for the data to kick in. There were times when the data did not kick in. When this occurred, we were usually glad that we had picked one of the top carriers because this made it easier to find a local store where we could get the matter resolved.

Next, consider the local information desk your best friend. Always check to see what local information is available about your new destination. If information is available, consider it reading material for your ride to your first night's accommodation. The information desk can also direct you to the local transportation to get to your destination/lodging.

Key Ingredients

Arrival Essentials:

- Minimize the time you spend standing in immigration lines by sitting as close to the front of the plane as possible, filling out your immigration cards while on the plane, and positioning yourselves by a door if you're being transported on a bus from the plane to the arrival terminal.
- Find an ATM to get some local currency.
- Buy a local carrier SIM card for your mobile phone.
- Gather a local map and travel brochures at the information kiosk.
- Find your transportation.

Where to Sleep – Lodging

Your home away from home is wherever you are spending the night. This can include: hotels, hostels, apartments, bed and breakfasts, a bedroom in someone's private home, lodges, tents, ships, trains or perhaps a bus. Each has its advantages and disadvantages. From a budget perspective, you should try to stretch your hotel points as far as you can. When we weren't using points, we tried to find a place for the equivalent of $100 or less per night. You can adjust this amount up or down according to your preference and budget. It is easier to stay within this budget when you research your potential accommodations online and you are aware of room rates, taxes, and fees for Wi-Fi and parking. You may have certain "must-haves" when looking for accommodations such as a fitness center, breakfast, kitchenette, or free Wi-Fi. Keep these in mind when conducting your searches.

One of our must-haves for lodging was having access to good Wi-Fi. Part of our search for lodging included reading reviews of the place to see if the Wi-Fi was any good and if the Wi-Fi was free or not. The quality of Wi-Fi service varied dramatically throughout the trip. We quickly learned that just because a place advertised that it had Wi-Fi service didn't mean that it worked well or that it was free. Sometimes, we could connect to a Wi-Fi network but the service was so painfully slow that it was virtually useless. Other times, there would be an additional charge to use the Wi-Fi, and in the worst scenario, there was an additional charge for each device that we connected and we had four of them (two tablets, one notebook, and one mobile phone).

Hotel

Hotels range from very basic budget on up through luxurious. To ensure you don't end up disappointed, we recommend you take the following steps:

Step 1: Check to see if there are any chain hotels in the area that offer "attractive" room rates using points for your stay.

What we mean by attractive is relative for each hotel chain. It seems like every year or two, hotel chains devalue their points by adding higher tiers that cost more and more points. If you're not careful, you can quickly blow through your points by paying too much. Through experience, we learned to seek out value when we used points, and we'll explain what we mean by that. There's also a hidden advantage to using reward points to pay for your room – you usually avoid having to pay local hotel taxes that can often add 15-25 percent to your hotel bill.

Here is what we recommend for the different hotel chains we've stayed in:

- **IHG Rewards Club:** IHG includes hotel chains such as Holiday Inn, Intercontinental, Crowne Plaza, and several others. We previously introduced you to IHG Rewards in our chapter on

"Saving Up," but the value of this program is so good that we want to cover it in more detail here. We made out like bandits by taking advantage of hotel rooms at IHG properties for just 5,000 points per night. First, we accumulated points in two ways: We each signed up for an IHG Rewards Points Credit Card and earned 60,000 bonus points each for a total of 120,000 points. Then, while we were on the road, IHG ran promotions where we could earn up to 50,000 more bonus points. Such promotions got our attention, and we would strategically plan just enough stays at IHG properties to earn the maximum bonus. That added up to 170,000 points, which gave us the potential for thirty-four free nights using PointBreaks rewards. And, that's mostly what we did with our points. We spent many a night in a Holiday Inn Express using points and took full advantage of the hotel's decent free breakfasts. IHG updates its PointBreaks offerings every sixty days. We set a reminder and jumped on reviewing the list as soon as it came out. We'd book several hotels right away to get them on our menu. Eventually, we ended up cancelling some of them as our travel took us elsewhere, but that wasn't a problem because there's no cancellation fee and the points are instantly credited back to your account. Some of the deals that we found were in countries that we wanted to visit but not cities that were on our menu. We booked some of these cities to get the deal and discovered some fascinating places that we otherwise wouldn't have visited such as Brno in the Czech Republic. We'd be remiss if we didn't give a shout out to www.extrapackofpeanuts.com for turning us on to this deal.

- **Hyatt:** We really came to love Hyatt hotels on this trip. Rich had amassed a lot of Hyatt points from business travel because his employer had negotiated favorable rates and required employees to stay at Hyatt properties. We found the Hyatt properties overseas to offer first-class accommodations. The sweet spot ranged between 10,000 to 15,000 points per night. We often booked two- to three-night stays when we were looking to pamper ourselves and found such rates available. We did not have a Hyatt credit card before we started the trip because it did not offer bonus points. Rather, it offers two free nights at *any* one of Hyatt's properties. Once we realized how much we were enjoying Hyatt's international hotel offerings, we decided to sign up for a Hyatt credit card using the address of Elizabeth's parents. They, in turn, sent us the card in one of their care packages. Given how much money we were spending on our trip, we quickly met the criteria to receive the two free nights, but we were patient about where to apply them. We found our chance when we visited London, where the hotel rates were somewhat astronomical. We stayed – for free – at a wonderful Hyatt hotel in London that would have cost us approximately $1,000 US if we were paying cash. We've already begun accumulating Hyatt points upon our return and can't wait to put them to good use in our future travels.

- **Marriott:** We had a lot of Marriott points built up, but we were disappointed with how expensive Marriott-branded properties are around the world. They often cost in excess of 25,000 points. Marriott does offer a free fifth night when you use points for the first four nights. We found the best value in Marriott's lesser-known chains like AC Hotels, where we were able to book rooms for 10,000 points per night. That enabled us to get five nights at a nice hotel for just 40,000 points, which for Marriott is about as good as it gets. In the time since we took our trip, Marriott has purchased Starwood. We hope Marriott doesn't merge with Starwood's fine program. Initially, Marriott plans to keep both programs around, but it is allowing members to transfer points from one program to the other, which is a nice perk.

- **Starwood:** We love Starwood properties. Starwood brands include Westin, Sheraton, Le Méridien, and others. We didn't have as many Starwood points built up. However, those that we did, we put to good use. We found some really good deals on Sheraton Hotels, getting some rooms for as little as 3,500 points. We also liked the option where Starwood offers discounted hotel room rates for a combination of points and cash. We used this on several occasions to stay at a nice hotel for a reasonable rate that usually saved us from the local hotel taxes, which can really add up. Starwood is one of the chains that also offers a free fifth night when you use points for the first four nights. That's another great way to stretch your points.

- **Hilton:** This is another hotel chain that offers a free fifth night when you stay four nights using points. We did not take advantage of this offer. However, similar to Starwood, Hilton also offers discounted room rates where you can use a combination of points and cash. We took advantage of such offers in Croatia and England. Hilton has some familiar brands including Doubletree and Hampton Inn, which we stayed at, as well as Embassy Suites. In general, we found Hilton properties to be rather expensive when using points. Thus, we had to be patient and wait until we found good value to stretch our points. We were rewarded for our patience when we stayed at our first

Hilton property, the Hilton Residences in Queenstown, New Zealand. It was one of our better scores on the trip.

- **Club Carlson:** Brands include Radisson, Park Inn, and a few others. If you sign up for a free Club Carlson account, you get free Internet when you stay at one of its properties, so make sure you sign up if there's a chance you might stay at one of its hotels. This is another chain that offers discounted hotel rates using a combination of points and cash, and we took advantage of it to stretch our points. We didn't have a whole lot of Club Carlson points to use, but we put what we had to good use staying at a Radisson on the outskirts of Milan and a Park Inn in Budapest that offered great value using points and cash.

The beauty of using a combination of points and dollars is that it can help you preserve your points and cut your daily budget on a room in half. Don't forget to keep your eye out for these deals. When you're looking at hotels, search for award travel on the various hotel websites that you have a points balance with. We also bought some hotel points along the way when we needed some extra points to have enough to make a reservation or when we found that it was actually cheaper to buy points and book with points than it was to pay cash for the room. Surprising as this is, it really does happen. It's also worth noting that some chains like Starwood will occasionally run promotions and sell their points at up to a 25 percent discount.

Step 2: After you've vetted the choices available using hotel points, research the hotel on TripAdvisor.

This is our favorite review site. It can be used around the world, will give you frank feedback from real people about the hotel, and generates an overall ranking and percentage recommended. Our general rule of thumb is to not book a room at a hotel with under 80 percent satisfaction. Another great TripAdvisor feature is that it gives you the price per night offered by several websites. Most of the time the hotel's actual website and Booking.com will give you the lowest rates. Trivago seems to be an up-and-comer that we became aware of toward the end of our trip. If you don't find a hotel with points, we recommend you check if any of the top hotels listed are within your budget and include the amenities you find important in your search criteria.

Step 3: Check the amenities.

Certain amenities can make or break your decision to choose a particular hotel. These may include: free Internet, free parking, air-conditioning, fitness center, free breakfast, in-room refrigerator, kettle, etc. As a traveler on the go, your number one amenity is probably going to be access to the Internet. Be sure to factor this and any other important amenities into your hotel search. TripAdvisor lets you select the amenities you want and then shows you only the hotels that include those amenities. If you like a hotel that doesn't have certain amenities such as free Wi-Fi and free parking, you can usually go directly to the hotel's site and see what the cost per day is. If you have status with the hotel chain, the hotel might waive these charges for you. In addition to determining what amenities the hotel offers, you should take one step further and look carefully to see what reviewers have to say. For example, there might be several reviewers that comment on the poor quality of the Internet or air-conditioning. We like to sleep under the covers in a cool room. While we're used to hotels in the USA that let us throttle the temperature up or down to our liking, it was hit or miss in hotels around the world. Many of the hotels that claimed to have air-conditioning kept it centrally controlled, making the thermostat in the room useless. Even though the hotel lists the amenity, it doesn't guarantee the quality. The extra step of checking reviews definitely requires more time and effort, but it's worth it to make sure that you enjoy your stays as much as possible.

Step 4: One final consideration for hotels is that we recommend you sign up for the rewards programs for the hotel chains that you're interested in staying at, even if you don't expect to build up any points before your trip.

The reason for this is that the hotel chains occasionally offer specials via email that are only available to members. They may offer a 20 percent discount or four nights for the price of three or something else that makes them more affordable than if you didn't belong to the program. You also get free Internet with programs such as Hilton Honors, Club Carlson, and others, and this can save you some money. Last but not least, programs such as IHG dangle tantalizing mega-bonus point goals at you if you stay more frequently at their properties. We found that some of the goals were well worth pursuing and helped to lower our overall cost per night by providing us with many additional free nights. We turned our 50,000 IHG bonus points into ten free nights using IHG's PointBreaks rewards. If you don't sign up for the programs, you'll never know about such great bonus opportunities.

The mention of the word "hostel" may conjure up an image of the basic youth hostel with rows of bunk beds. While you will often find this type of sleeping arrangement, many hostels offer ensuites (includes a private bathroom) or a private room with a shared bathroom. Hostels typically have common spaces such as lounge areas and kitchens for guests to share. This provides better opportunities for social interaction with other guests, who often enjoy swapping travel experience stories.

Some of the tradeoffs of staying at a hostel versus a hotel are that the guest rooms tend to be smaller and can be somewhat claustrophobic. They are often bare bones and therefore do not supply the basic amenities (like towels, soap, etc.) that we take for granted in a hotel. There usually is no maid service during multinight stays. Wi-Fi can be less reliable than in hotels and often only works in the common areas and not in the guest rooms. Hostels can also be a bit noisier as they tend to attract a younger clientele that likes to stay out late and party.

Two great sites we used to find and book a hostel are: www.hostelbookers.com and www.hostelworld.com. Here you can use their search engines to bring up a list of all the hostels in the area. Keep in mind that the price shown is per person. So, what may look like a great deal will actually be double the cost for two people. These sites show a percentage rating and number of reviews. We typically used 80 percent favorable as the cutoff and made sure there were more than thirty reviews. We always read the most recent reviews to better understand the age of the people who stayed there and what they liked and didn't like. If several reviews complimented the bar and nearness to clubs, we would usually avoid that hostel and find a quieter place, which had a better chance of delivering an uninterrupted night of sleep. We learned this lesson during our last night in Osaka, Japan, when a rowdy group of guys rolled in at about 3:30a.m. and continued the party in the bunkroom next door to us. We had to get up early the next morning to catch a flight. Needless to say, we had difficulty falling back asleep and were somewhat annoyed.

The biggest advantage of a hostel is its lower cost, which helps tremendously when you're trying to stretch a travel budget. However, we like to get comfortable and chill out in our room in the evening, surfing the Internet to plan the next leg of our trip. When faced with small rooms and unpredictable Wi-Fi performance, we tended to shy away from hostels as we got deeper and deeper into the trip.

Apartment

We define an apartment as an accommodation that includes a self-catering kitchen. It might be a studio or have one bedroom or more. It might be found within a private home, an apartment hotel, an apartment building, or a multifamily house.

This is our favorite type of accommodation when staying somewhere for more than three days because it feels more like home. Apartments provided us with more living space and allowed us to establish a more normal routine. When staying in apartments, we often made our own breakfast, lunch, and dinner, which was fairly economical when compared to eating out. We usually had decent air-conditioning and good Wi-Fi. Daily maid service is usually provided only in apartment hotels. In a number of rentals, we got to know the owners a little bit, and they willingly shared insights about the location where we were staying. A few of the buildings included a fitness center, which was a nice bonus. Many also provided parking at no extra charge.

The problem with finding apartments is that they are not always easy to search for. TripAdvisor has four categories of accommodation on its site: Hotels, B&Bs and Inns, Specialty Lodging, and Vacation Rentals. Most likely, you will find apartments and apartment hotels under Specialty Lodging. Once you've narrowed the search to Specialty Lodging, we recommend you use the amenities filter and select Kitchenette to make sure you'll have a kitchen.

Another option to finding an apartment is to use sites such as Homeaway.com, VRBO, AirBNB, or TripAdvisor's Vacation Rental link, which is powered by a company called FlipKey. These sites allow owners to list their apartments, and you can book directly with the owner online. You can see ratings and reviews, but there probably won't be as many reviews as you'll find for standard hotels. So, you may be taking more of a gamble here. One last place to look is Booking.com. Many independent owners use this site because it doesn't charge fees and is easy to use and maintain.

Bed and Breakfast/Inn

We didn't stay at many bed and breakfasts or inns until the latter part of our trip because we're fairly unpredictable in the morning and didn't want to be boxed in to a pre-arranged meal at a fixed time. However, once we stayed at them with greater frequency, we really enjoyed our stays.

B&Bs usually provide a private room with bathroom (our preference), although sometimes you will be sharing a bathroom. Given the name, breakfast is always provided, and it is often cooked to order. Depending on the owner, breakfast can vary from a simple spread to an elaborate feast. We aren't big breakfast eaters – a bowl of cereal, some yogurt, and fruit is a typical breakfast for us, but if you like a cooked breakfast, this type of accommodation can be a real treat. Usually, you will need to let the owner know the night before what time you'd like breakfast and what items you will be selecting from the menu. This is what was tough for us because on nontravel days we don't like to have a rigid schedule. Staying at a B&B forced us to get up and eat at a particular time. On the bright side, we were able to meet other travelers at breakfast and get to know the owners better.

We found the B&B owners to be friendly and full of good local sightseeing advice. Daily maid service was not common on multiday stays. Our favorite B&Bs were the ones that offered a dinner option. We had some fantastic dinners offered by the hosts at reasonable prices that we still talk about today. The Wi-Fi was hit or miss at the B&Bs. This was less of a problem later in the trip; by that time, we'd gotten pretty good at using our mobile phone as a hotspot and backup plan. The main downsides to B&Bs were that many lacked air-conditioning and the price point was often higher than our preferred pricing.

Once again, TripAdvisor and Booking.com were our go-to sources for finding bed and breakfast stays. Many B&Bs may have reviews on TripAdvisor but only allow you to book a room through their website, so don't get discouraged if TripAdvisor says, "Contact accommodation for availability." Google the name of the B&B and visit its website where you can either book online or call. This was the case for almost all of the places we stayed at in Scotland. You may find a place on AirBNB, but mostly these are just a spare room in someone's home or a studio apartment, neither of which include the traditional breakfast.

Friend's Place

The most economical form of accommodation is when you can stay in an extra bedroom in someone's home for free. Our good friends, Ann and Adam, put us up for a few nights at their beautiful new home on the Gold Coast of Australia. This was a real treat; it was like staying at a resort. However, this was the only place that we visited where we had good friends that we could mooch off of. We used AirBNB to rent a bedroom in someone's private home in Australia. While we found this to be economical and more social, it was just a bit too far outside of our comfort zone and we didn't pursue this type of accommodation again.

Lodge/Tent

You are most likely going to find this kind of accommodation in parks. We stayed at lodges and in "luxury" tents during our safari in Uganda. We were able to see reviews about the different accommodations on TripAdvisor and adjusted some of our stays with our travel company based on what we read. Given where we were, our accommodations were quite nice, but compared to what we are used to, this was roughing it for us. The "luxury" tents were one-bedroom, semi-permanent tents with two twin beds and a bathroom and shower off the back. The lodges were wooden one-room bedrooms with modern toilets and showers. There was no air-conditioning, and we slept under mosquito nets as a precaution due to the risk of malaria. The days were hot and the nights were cool, but it took a while for our sleeping quarters to cool off making it more difficult for us to fall asleep. Running water was hard to come by. So, we usually washed and showered with gravity-fed water. Some places provided daily maid service, while others did not.

Ironically, Rich ran into an old gym friend at one of our luxury tent camps in Uganda. One morning while having breakfast under a tent, one of the guests pointed at Rich and yelled out, "I know I know you from somewhere." It turns out that Ram Iyer and Rich had befriended each other in a New Jersey gym, where they exercised together in the mornings but hadn't seen each other in over a dozen years. Ram is an accomplished world traveler and photographer. If you're looking for some travel inspiration, check out Ram's blog at http://ramdasiyer.travellerspoint.com. It's a small world after all.

Cruise Ship

We must admit that taking an extended cruise holds no appeal for us. We know lots of people who love cruises, and we're happy for them. It's just not the way that we like to roll. That said, we did travel overnight by ship from Helsinki, Finland to Saint Petersburg, Russia, and then a few days later returned on an overnight crossing of the Gulf of Finland. We had an internal cabin, which was great because it was pitch black when we turned out the lights. The ride was fairly smooth, but we were concerned that the gentle rocking might keep us awake. So, just to be safe, we took a sleeping pill (a generic equivalent of Ambien) and slept like babies both ways. The air-conditioning was good, but the Wi-Fi was poor and expensive, which came as no surprise. The bars and restaurants on the ship were also good. We found travel by ship to be reasonable in price because we were combining the costs of transportation and lodging in one fare.

Plane

We spent a few nights on planes on overnight flights including our initial flight to China. When this occurred and the flight was at least eight hours long, we usually took a sleeping pill to help get a decent night's rest. The eye shades and ear plugs that we brought along also came in handy as there's always some undesired noise and light to contend with on long flights.

Train

As we mentioned earlier, we could have taken an overnight train from Beijing to Xi'an but we opted for a much quicker high-speed train during the day. We did have a sleeper compartment for our return trip from Agra to Delhi during the day and Elizabeth took advantage of it to take a nap. We also enjoyed the privacy as we had the compartment all to ourselves.

Bus

Finally, we spent a night on a bus as part of a twenty-hour trip from Salta to Mendoza, Argentina. Using a mix of English and Spanish, it was fairly easy to book the bus fare at the local bus station. We did this, of all nights, on New Year's Eve. We were curious as to whether the atmosphere would be festive or not on the bus. It turned out to be quiet and peaceful, which was fine with us. After wishing each other a Happy New Year, we downed a sleeping pill to help ensure a good night's rest and to pass some time. Once again, it worked like a charm for both of us. (Before you begin to think that we're dependent upon sleeping pills, we're not. We strategically use them as a travel aid when it makes sense. Over the course of the year, we used about a dozen pills each.)

Getting back to the bus, we paid for the better class of service and found the seats to be extremely comfortable. It was like we each had our own leather reclining lounger. Going into the trip, we were somewhat dreading a twenty-hour bus ride. Coming out of it, we'd definitely do it again in a place like Argentina where the buses are designed for long-distance travel and the roadways are good.

There were a couple of drawbacks, though. The bus was a bit on the warm side, and there was nothing we could do about it. We just had to endure it. We also had to stow our backpacks in the bus's cargo hold. The bus made several stops along the route where passengers embarked and disembarked. This put our bags at risk of being stolen. Fortunately, they weren't. However, they were wet and dirty by the time we reached our destination. This was the result of thunderstorms that were so bad the bus pulled over for about an hour until they passed. Meanwhile, the skies opened up and the rain came down in torrents. This made a mess in the cargo hold where our backpacks were stored. We weren't happy, but we got over it. All in all, bus travel offered great value when compared to air travel in Argentina. And, we saved a night's accommodation costs while traveling to our destination.

Key Ingredients

Where to Sleep – Lodging:

- Establish a budget for your average room cost per night.
- Prepare your list of "must haves" when looking for accommodations such as a fitness center, breakfast, kitchenette, or free Wi-Fi.

Hotel:

- If you have accumulated hotel reward points, identify what price in points offers good value and see if there are any hotels where you're interested in staying that offer good value using points. Here are examples of where we found good value:

- IHG Rewards – Look for PointBreaks deals for 5,000 points/night.
- Hyatt – We found the sweet spot to be 10,000-15,000 points/ night.
- Starwood – We like its offers to use a combination of points and cash. For longer stays, it offers five nights for the price of four when you use points.
- Marriott – We found the best value in its lesser-known brands such as AC Hotels. Marriott also offers five nights for the price of four when using points.
- Hilton – You need to be patient until a good value comes along. You'll know it when you see it. This is another program that offers five nights for the price of four when you use points.
- Club Carlson – We like this chain's offers to use a combination of points and cash along with free Internet for members.
- Check out a hotel's reviews on TripAdvisor before making your final selection.
- Make a list of amenities that you prefer and use filters on websites that offer them to quickly narrow the results to hotels that meet your needs.
- Sign up for the rewards programs of hotels that you enjoy staying at and subscribe to their email offers.

Hostel:

- Consult www.hostelbookers.com and www.hostelworld.com. Both are good search engines for hostels.

Apartment:

- Look for apartments on sites such as TripAdvisor (under Specialty Lodging), HomeAway, VRBO, AirBNB, and Booking.com.

Bed and Breakfast/Inn:

- Find B&Bs on TripAdvisor and Booking.com, our go-to sources for B&Bs.

Friend's Place:

- If your budget is tight, get a little help from friends. This is a great way to save money. Friends of friends may also be eager to host you.

Lodge/Tent:

- Lodges may include breakfast and dinner. Take this into account when evaluating the higher cost of this type of accommodation.

Ship:

- Do your travel planning in advance of boarding your vessel. Wi-Fi is likely to be expensive and poor on the ship.

Plane/Bus:

- Make sure that you have eye shades, earplugs, and possibly an inflatable neck roll to help you sleep. For long overnight travel, consider a sleeping pill.

What To See and Do

Now that you have your transportation and accommodations situated, what are you going to do at your next travel destination? While you may have made plans for what you want to see and do before you arrive at your destination (for example: seeing the Taj Mahal in Agra or trekking the Great Wall in China), there may be things you never dreamed of seeing or doing that, with a little extra research, can open your eyes to some truly special adventures. We suggest you do three things during your trip to help enhance what you see and do: utilize your online resources, listen to fellow travelers and hosts, and leverage the local tourist information office.

Utilize Your Online Resources

Internet Forums: There are abundant online resources on topics pertaining to what you can see and do on your trip. Whether you are searching for your next destination or have just arrived and need suggestions, there are several places we suggest you check out for inspiration. We mention TripAdvisor in the sleeping and eating sections, but we also think its travel forums offer a diverse selection under the "Things to do" section for each city/region. This is user-driven with personal recommendations and advice. Since the activities are in order of the top to bottom rated, this is an easy way to look through what others are highlighting. Another useful link within TripAdvisor is its actual Travel Forum (www.tripadvisor.com/ForumHome). These sections are set up at the regional and city level so if you aren't exactly sure where to visit in the south of France, you can search the regional forums for advice and then narrow down your search once you have selected a few cities to focus on. These travel forums usually have up-to-date information about any concerns you care to address (e.g., recent terrorist activity or financial crisis) as well as upcoming events.

Aside from TripAdvisor, other online resources we recommend include: Yelp (www.yelp.com), another consumer-driven resource full of advice and reviews from fellow travelers; local city tourism websites often in the form of www.cityname.com such as www.budapest.com; and Ticketmaster (www.ticketmaster.com) if you're looking for concert, theater, or sporting events.

Online Magazines and Guidebooks: A subscription to your local library can prove handy if your library has an online portal for downloading magazines and travel books for free. We found *Frommer's Travel Guides* and guides by Rick Steves to be the most popular options for the countries we visited. The online version might not be as easy to read and reference as a print book, but it will save you having to lug around a lot of hefty books. If you can't find a guidebook through your library, you can always buy one from Amazon Kindle or iBooks. Read the reviews before making the investment in these books as the costs can add up. *Time Out* magazine (www.timeout.com) is a good resource for upcoming events and trendy restaurants, is written for many places around the world, and is translated into many languages.

Listen to Fellow Travelers and Hosts

You are likely to run into many other travelers during your trip. A great place to meet other tourists is at hostels, on group tours, and at tourist attractions (like while waiting in line to gain access to a popular museum). Step out of your comfort zone, strike up a conversation, and ask people for recommendations on some of their favorite places to visit and what they suggest to see and do. You might not act upon their recommendations, but you never know what is going to spark your interest and alter your plans. Regardless of how many online forums and articles you read, it is helpful to get a real perspective on someone's recent travels. We have many fellow travelers to thank for inspiring us to visit unique places, try restaurants we never would have considered, and book excursions that turned out to be fascinating.

One of the advantages of staying at a bed and breakfast is that the hosts are usually eager to give you the lay of the land and provide an insider's take on their city and country. They are excellent resources for discovering the best restaurants in the area as well as some off-the-beaten-path places to tour. If you're staying in a hotel, seek out the concierge for his or her recommendations.

Leverage the Local Tourist Information Office

Government- or state-run tourist information offices are fantastic resources to help point you in the direction for what to see and do. They have experts on their local area and often have the most up-to-date information for what's going on and what's popular. Some countries might have such an office in every city; whereas in other places you might be hard pressed to find any tourist information offices at all. When you can find them, use them. They typically have good maps and self-guided walking tours to help you get a sense of the city on your own.

Tours

We used tours sparingly because they added to the cost of our trip. However, we liked to scan what tour operators were highlighting in an area. This gave us ideas for our own sightseeing adventures. When we did arrange a tour, we often turned to Viator (www.viator.com), which offered a nice selection of tours around the world. This company partners with local tour operators. We found Viator tours to be reasonably priced and consistently good. Its website and mobile app were fun to browse and included numerous reviews that we would always read before booking a tour. As an example, we used Viator to book a tour of the Vatican museum while in Rome, and it definitely enhanced our experience. Our tour guide was a wealth of information.

What to Eat and Drink

Sampling a variety of food and drink from around the world added a lot of spice to our life. While we wouldn't call ourselves the most adventurous eaters in the world, we did occasionally step out of our comfort zone, and when we did, we were rewarded with some incredible meals. We like to try and eat healthy, but that wasn't always possible. We're typically cautious when it comes to eating street food, but we ate some in places where we never thought we would and we're glad we did. We had memorable meals in faraway places that topped anything we'd ever experienced before. We also ate in our room quite a bit and lost count of how many different supermarkets we visited. In this chapter, we'll give you a sense of eating out vs. eating in for breakfast, lunch, and dinner. We won't bore you with the details of all of the different foods that we ate. Instead, we'll provide a sampling of the highlights. If you're interested in learning more, each of our blog posts on www. ourtravelmenu.com includes a section on food and drink.

Let's be honest, one of the fears that most world travelers have is getting traveler's diarrhea from something they ate. We share this fear, and quite frankly, we expected it to happen sooner or later. Thus, we made sure to bring a prescription of antibiotics (ten pills of Ciprofloxacin HCL 500mg) to take in case we came down with it. Luckily, neither of us had to take it. That's not to say that we didn't have some stomach issues along the way. We each suffered some intestinal problems, but they never seemed to last more than twenty-four to thirty-six hours and it rarely happened to us at the same time or became extreme. We like to share just about everything we eat. Yet, our stomachs seemed to be sensitive to different foods. We consider ourselves most fortunate, but we can say from experience that it is possible to travel the world for an extended period without contracting the dreaded traveler's diarrhea.

We've divided this section into eating out and eating in for each main meal of the day. We hope this helps you with your options on the road.

Eating Out

Eating Out – Breakfast: A great bang for your buck is to stay at a hotel that includes free breakfast. You will consistently find this amenity available in some chain hotels such as Holiday Inn Express, but we also found a number of independent hotels offering a free breakfast. The most common format of service is buffet style. The range of options will vary dramatically in offering and quality, but most buffets will include a minimum of breads, sliced meats, cheese, fruit, yogurt, and cereal. They might also offer baked goods and hot foods such as eggs, bacon, beans, and vegetables. We also received free breakfast when we stayed at a hotel where we had status in the hotel's rewards program. For example, Marriott hotels usually had a club lounge with a complimentary breakfast buffet that we'd be provided access to. Many of the B&Bs that we stayed at offered cooked-to-order breakfasts including eggs, bacon, ham, smoked salmon, pancakes, toast, jams, and more. When breakfast wasn't provided but we felt like eating out, we usually chose a quaint breakfast place where we could order a satisfying warm breakfast or pastry. We'd be remiss if we didn't give a shout out to the Eastin Grand Hotel Sathorn in Bangkok, Thailand, for the most amazing free breakfast buffet we've ever had the pleasure of feasting on. We were served an indescribable assortment of scrumptious hot and cold international foods that were without compare.

Eating Out – Lunch: If you travel like us, your day-to-day schedule will be unpredictable and depend on what time you wake up. Normally, this wouldn't be a problem in the States, but in many countries around the world, businesses close for siesta in the afternoon. Thus, restaurants will often close by 2 or 3p.m. Keep in mind that if you sleep in and have a late breakfast, you can easily get shut out for lunch and left without any options until dinner.

It was rare for us to eat out for both lunch and dinner. So, when we did go out for lunch, we usually made it our big meal of the day. Throughout Europe, many restaurants offer a plate of the day or as the French like to call it: *plat du jour*. These are attractively priced two- or three-course meals. They offer good food and good value when compared to the price of dinner. We took advantage of quite a few of these deals and would combine them with a house wine and turn them into what we fondly referred to as "Happy Meals." After our Happy Meal, we would head back to our lodging and take a nap just like the locals often do.

The most interesting lunch that we ate occurred early in our trip in Xi'an, China. We ordered a chicken dish and a pork dish to share. Since both were light on vegetables, we also ordered a dish of donkey and cauliflower just to get the cauliflower. As it turned out, the chicken had bones and parts that we wouldn't typically eat, and the pork was served in the form of thick and greasy bacon-like strips. However, the donkey was boneless and had the characteristics we were expecting in the chicken and pork. We tried it and, much to our surprise, we really liked it. Hence, we abandoned the chicken and pork and finished off the donkey.

Eating Out – Dinner: You may enjoy going out to dinner at a nice restaurant with white tablecloths like we do at home. However, on the road, you might not have the appropriate attire to eat in fancy restaurants nor want to spend a lot of money on dinner. So, before hitting the streets, we recommend you check out TripAdvisor, which is a reliable resource for casual restaurants throughout the world. Another suggestion is to seek out advice from locals on where they like to eat. We'd much rather eat where the locals eat than where the tourists eat.

Given a choice, we prefer eating dinner around 7p.m. In many countries, however, restaurants don't open until 8p.m., so we had to adapt accordingly. You may be more accustomed to eating later and won't have as much trouble adapting. We found it funny that if we showed up at 8p.m., the restaurants would usually be empty and people would just start to roll in as we were leaving. Occasionally, we did a restaurant crawl in which we'd each get an appetizer to share and a glass of wine at the bar and then move on to the next place and repeat the process. This was a fun way to get a better sense of the local cuisine. We had the most fun doing this in the form of tapas crawls in Spain's Rioja wine country.

We were really wary about eating street food for fear of unsanitary conditions that would lead to sickness. However, we read many travel blogs where people raved about how delicious and inexpensive street food was in different locations. This inspired us to give it a try, and we hope you do, too. That's not to say that everything was good. It wasn't. But, the street food tended to be so inexpensive, that if we really didn't like something, we would move on and try something else.

The best street food that we had was at the night markets in China where we explored on our own and used a lot of improvised sign language to get what we wanted. Once we thought that we were ordering a simple dish of new potatoes, only to watch the street vendor add about seven different spices to the frying pan before cooking the potatoes. The end result coated our mouths with scintillating taste sensations that we'll never forget. As we recall, this tasty treat cost us the equivalent of less than one dollar. We never thought that we'd be eating street food in India, but we did so as part of a guided walking tour of the old city in New Delhi. Once again, the food was delicious and inexpensive. We didn't make a habit of eating street food, but we did find it to be an entertaining experience when we did.

Similar to breakfast, some of the larger hotel chains, where we had status in their rewards program, offered complimentary hot and cold foods to their members in their club lounges. In some cases, the food was so good that we turned it into dinner. That was the case when we used points in the IHG Rewards program to stay at the Intercontinental Hotel in Santiago, Chile. Not only did we receive free food but free drinks, too, which was a nice bonus.

Eating In

We have become supermarket aficionados of sorts. We love to scout out supermarkets everywhere we travel to see what familiar products, if any, they might have and to get a sense of what our eating-in options might be. When we found a good supermarket, we might visit it two or even three times a day if it was conveniently located. This may sound crazy, but we might make a run in the morning to pick something up for breakfast, then later to buy fixings for lunch, and then again in the evening to purchase dinner items. If we didn't find what we were looking for at one supermarket, we'd seek out another one. We probably spent way too much time in supermarkets, but it did give us an idea of what the locals liked to eat. In most countries, there were a reasonable number of American brands that we were familiar with. The one exception was Japan. Aside from consistently good bakery items, we really struggled to find suitable products to purchase for our consumption there.

It's worth noting that various forms of farmers' markets can be found all around the world. They offer fresh fruit, vegetables, cheeses, prepared foods, and other items that have a local flair. We became especially fond of the indoor markets in France, which can be found in most larger towns and cities. We took full advantage of these markets to buy delicious foods for breakfast, lunch, and dinner. The food in France is "evil-good" meaning that it's so good that it's evil. We spent about five weeks in France and figure that we gained at least five pounds each, but we enjoyed every bite along the way.

Eating In – Breakfast: When we're at home, a typical breakfast consists of a bowl of cereal or a granola bar, a small dish of plain nonfat yogurt, and a banana or some other fruit. So, it'll come as no surprise that this is what we often ate on the road. We were disappointed that one of our mainstay cereals, Cheerios, was unavailable most of the time. We took a liking to Fitness, which is similar to Special K but we like it even better. Yogurt styles can vary quite a bit, and each country has its own brands and styles, many of which seemed really "soupy" to us. Rich got excited when we'd find his favorite, Fage Greek Yogurt, which wasn't often. We could always find bananas, but they varied in size and taste. As we said, we like to eat healthy, but there are so many temptations on the road. Some of them, such as bakeries, got the best of us more than we care to say. There are excellent bakeries all over the world, even in places like China where we didn't expect to find them. And, then there's Japan, where the fresh baked goodies seemed to be everywhere. Consequently, there was many a morning where we made a bakery run and indulged ourselves in whatever caught our eye, and we were rarely disappointed.

Eating In – Lunch: The most common lunch for us was sandwiches because they're so portable. Peanut butter and honey, which didn't need to be refrigerated, became a staple for us. The downside was that since we weren't checking our backpacks when we flew, we often had to toss the sandwich spreads before we finished them. Still, they were quite economical, and we were able to find sliced wholewheat bread in most places. To change things up, we occasionally bought lunchmeat, sliced cheese, and mustard, but this was usually when we had a refrigerator in our room. Once we visited France, we switched over to French baguette sandwiches that were far and away the most satisfying. For us, the bread in France is as good as it gets. Stores even sell sliced cheese that is specifically sized for baguette sandwiches. Include some reduced-fat potato chips, cookies, and apples and we had a delicious lunch. We'd throw everything into one of our daypacks with some water, head off on a hike, and find an inviting spot to have a picnic.

Eating In – Dinner: You would think that eating in is a good way to save money. For us, however, sometimes it was and sometimes it wasn't. We seemed to do best in the savings department when we cooked. This isn't our favorite thing to do, but when we had a decent kitchen setup to work with, we often took advantage of it. We have a good recipe for pasta primavera that we'll sometimes add chicken to. When we made it with a full box of pasta, we always had leftovers, which we'd stretch into two or maybe even three meals. We also found rotisserie chicken to be available in quite a few countries. We sautéed the chicken with some vegetables, microwaved a bag of rice, and voila, we had another dinner. You may not consider this cooking, but it is for us, given our limited skills. We often warmed up the leftover chicken the next night and added it to a fresh salad.

When we didn't have a proper kitchen to cook in, which was most of the time, we prepared a cold smorgasbord that would include hard and soft cheese; fresh veggies like broccoli, cauliflower, carrots, plum tomatoes, and more with hummus or some other dip; a protein such as smoked salmon, sliced ham, turkey, chicken, or shrimp; and French bread or crackers. We supplemented this assortment with other foods such as olives, potato chips, almonds, etc. Another eat-in option for us was take-out food. We bought Chinese, Thai, pizza, and sushi, and brought it back to our room. Sometimes, when we were feeling lazy, we'd even have it delivered.

It's worth mentioning that we carried our own utensils in the form of plastic spoons, forks, and knives, which we picked up at take-out food places. We washed them and reused them until they broke, then replaced them when the opportunity presented itself. These utensils came in handy on many occasions.

It's important to have snack foods with you to munch on when you're hungry and on the go or winding down at night. Our go-to foods included graham crackers, apples, almonds, cashews, granola bars, potato chips, pretzels, rice crackers, and almond crackers. Of course, with the exception of apples, it was hit or miss as to whether we'd find these products or not. So, we'd have to adapt our tastes to what was available. As an example, graham crackers were hard to come by, so we switched over to Digestives. One amusing note is that we made the mistake of assuming that the price of apples was pretty standard around the world. Imagine then, our surprise when we paid $20 for four apples at a supermarket in Seoul, South Korea.

Drinking

Here is a warning regarding this section. We have a fondness for alcoholic beverages, especially wine, which we go into some detail in this section. We recognize that alcoholic beverages are not for everyone, and that's just fine. We respect people's right to enjoy whatever they choose. We've provided the information on what we like to give you a sense of how we took advantage of travel to further explore our interests in wine and spirits. You may have entirely different interests. One of the pleasures of world travel is being able to explore your interests and allow them to influence the destinations that you choose, just as we did with our passion for wine.

Water: Drinking the local tap water presents the highest risk for getting sick. The water may be safe for the locals to drink because their systems are acclimated to it, but tourists, like you, might run into trouble if you drink it. Thus, we suggest you become vigilant in researching a country's water safety before arriving (see the "Pre-arrival" chapter). When in doubt, avoid tap water. In some countries, you shouldn't even brush your teeth with it. Avoid drinks with ice when you are in a country with questionable tap water, unless you have assurances that bottled water was used to make the ice. The good news is that there is inexpensive bottled water in abundant supply around the world. For the sake of convenience, we usually bought water in large bottles of one liter or more and used them to refill smaller bottles, which we carried around with us. Once or twice a week, we replaced our smaller disposable bottles for hygienic purposes. One trick that we learned is that many hotel gyms have a purified water dispenser. We often took advantage of them to refill our large water bottles. It saved a little money and a few trips to the supermarket.

In many countries, sparkling water is quite popular, but it can be a challenge distinguishing still from sparkling water in foreign languages. On more than one occasion, we bought the wrong one. It wasn't the end of the world as we enjoy sparkling water and would often drink it with dinner. Just for fun, while we were in France, we decided to conduct a blind taste test of sparkling waters. Much to our surprise, the winner was Perrier followed by the generic store brand. Our favorite going in, or so we thought, was a popular Italian brand, but it came in last. To be fair, we only conducted this taste test once. We'll have to do it again someday to see if we get similar results. Of course, your tastes may be completely different from ours.

Tea: Tea is readily available just about everywhere in the world. Many accommodations provide an electric hot pot to heat water to a boil. In countries where the water was risky, we used bottled water in the hot pot. The selection of teas offered was based on local preferences.

Elizabeth developed a fondness for Earl Grey tea, which we stocked up on and brewed when the local choices weren't as appealing.

Coffee: Like many Americans, Rich prefers filtered coffee, but that was hard to come by in many parts of the world where espresso drinks dominate. The next best option is a cafe Americano, which is a shot or two of espresso with some steaming hot water added. The challenge, we found, was trying to figure out what this drink was called in each country. For example, the equivalent drink in Australia is called a "Long Black." In hindsight, it might have been nice to have packed a French press designed for travel in our gear along with some ground coffee to satisfy Rich's cravings when even espresso was hard to come by.

Milk: We're used to buying fresh milk in the refrigerated section of supermarkets in the USA. However, that's not the case in most other countries that we visited. Instead, milk is processed and packaged so that it has a long shelf life and doesn't have to be refrigerated until it's opened. While we didn't do a side-by-side taste comparison, we're happy to report that we couldn't tell the difference. The warm milk off the shelf tasted just fine.

Juice: We found fruit juices available at just about all of the breakfasts that we were served. Orange juice was universally popular and consistently outstanding in Morocco.

Wines of the World
___

We are passionate about wine, and we made a point to visit major wine-producing regions around the world. It was tough starting out in Asia, where wine selection is both limited and expensive. As a result, we found ourselves drinking more beer than wine there. Once we arrived in Australia, things quickly changed and we enjoyed delicious regional wines in Australia, New Zealand, Argentina, Chile, South Africa, Portugal, Italy, France, and Spain. The UK imports wines from all over the world, so we continued to enjoy good wines at reasonable prices there as well. We find that wine tastes better in wineglasses. Since most of the places we stayed in didn't have wineglasses, we purchased an inexpensive set of wineglasses in Argentina and they accompanied us for the rest of our trip. Given that we love wine so much, here's a brief overview of our experiences by region:

Australia: The Margaret River region south of Perth on the west coast disappointed us. We previously had a similar experience in the Hunter Valley north of Sydney. However, the exceptional wines being produced in the southeast near Adelaide, a city that we're quite fond of, more than made up for these disappointments. The regions of Barossa, McLaren Vale, and Adelaide Hills stood out. Shiraz (Syrah) is what they're most known for, but we enjoyed several other red varietals from these regions. The only downside was that the wines were more expensive than most wine regions we've visited.

New Zealand: We love Sauvignon Blanc from the Marlborough region, and you can't beat the price. We also enjoy Pinot Noir from Central Otago, but it's a bit expensive.

Argentina: Mendoza is the largest wine-producing region in Argentina, but the town lacked the charm that we had envisioned and felt more like an industrial production wine zone. The area also has a way to go to improve its wine tourism. That said, this region does produce fine malbecs at reasonable prices. The highlight for us was Cafayate, which claims to be the highest elevation major wine-producing region in the world. We enjoyed the white Torrontés varietal along with Cabernet Sauvignon and Malbec there.

Chile: Chile made a great impression on us with the quality and value that its wines offered. We discovered many good wines for under $10 a bottle. We especially enjoyed Chardonnay from the Casablanca region and found good Carménère and Cabernet Sauvignon from areas such as Colchagua.

South Africa: Similar to Chile, we found a lot of good, inexpensive wine in South Africa. The Chenin Blanc was refreshing, and the red blends seemed to stand out from the single varietals. Wine critics in the USA often bash Pinotage. However, we happened upon several that we liked.

Portugal: There's an abundance of inexpensive wine available, but it's intended for food pairing and not our favorite wine just on its own. Some good red blends are coming out of the Douro River Valley, but you have to be selective and these are not cheap. The value can be found in the white Vinho Verde wines. They have a slight effervescence to them and are quite refreshing. Then, there's the Port that Portugal is most famous for. This is a fortified wine which is often served after dinner. There are several different styles of Port. Our favorites were twenty-year-old tawny and vintage Port.

Italy: We found a new favorite wine region in Veneto where Valpolicella is produced. We had a false impression that Valpolicella is an inexpensive, mass production wine. To the contrary, Italy has several high-quality, small producers making delicious, reasonably priced wine that's ready to drink now. There were lots of good wines in Tuscany, but as in Australia, the price tags were considerably higher. We also enjoyed Nero d'Avola in Sicily.

France: The Rhône Valley and Bordeaux offer several good wines. We cared less for the wines of the Loire Valley where Cabernet Franc dominates. We found that wines varied considerably from producer to producer, and there are so many producers that we had trouble finding the wines we liked in the stores. The biggest discovery for us in France is that there are a number of cooperatives where growers combine their grapes and the "coop" then produces the wines. Many of the coops offered free tastings of their reasonably priced wines. Once we discovered coops in Bordeaux, we sought them out during the rest of our time in France and enjoyed some nice inexpensive wines.

Spain: We love the red wines of Rioja, which are predominantly Tempranillo. These wines offer excellent value for the money. The alcohol levels are usually quite reasonable at 13.0 to 13.5 percent, which is the way we prefer it.

We'd be negligent if we didn't mention the challenges we had traveling with a *corkscrew*. While some airport security checkpoints paid no attention to our simple corkscrews designed for travel, others confiscated them. We had at least half a dozen corkscrews confiscated along the way until we found a molded plastic corkscrew at a hotel in

Sicily. We found another one in France. They accompanied us for the remainder of the trip and worked well enough to get the job done.

Sparkling Wine: Every now and then, we like to share a sparkling wine. We made a visit to the Champagne region of France that was well worth the trip. We also shared a bottle of Champagne at the Royal Ascot horse race meeting in England, where bottled Champagne is the only alcoholic beverage that fans are permitted to bring into the track. That would never be allowed in the USA, not in "bottles" anyway. The highlight for us, however, was tasting sparkling Shiraz from Samuel's Gorge winery in the McLaren Vale region of South Australia.

Beer: We found the best beers in Europe, but the beers were good everywhere we went, especially throughout Asia. If we had to pick a favorite, it would have to be Staropramen in the Czech Republic, where beer is known as "pivo."

Spirits: We also enjoy some spirits and cocktails once in a while. Occasionally, we sampled the local spirit of choice in a country. As an example, pisco is both popular and potent in Peru and commonly served in a pisco sour. The El Albergue hotel that we stayed at in Oliantayambo offered two-for-one specials during happy hour, and this offer lured us in more than once. In France, we made a side trip to the area of Cognac and toured Hennessy's facility. These fine spirits stand out on their own, but they also mix well with ginger ale. The best spirits of the trip, however, were found in Scotland where we finished up our trip. We gained a real appreciation for single malt scotch whisky and found the sweet spot to be those aged between fourteen and eighteen years. Elizabeth's favorite was the Balvenie fourteen-year-old Caribbean Cask while Rich preferred the Bowmore 18. Much to our surprise, we discovered a gin being produced there called The Botanist that is the best we've ever had.

Key Ingredients

What to Eat and Drink:

- Be prepared and get a prescription from a doctor for an antibiotic before you leave, such as Ciprofloxacin, to treat traveler's diarrhea.

Eating Out – Breakfast:

- See if your hotel offers a free breakfast buffet. Consider this as a preferred amenity when searching for hotels.

Eating Out – Lunch:

- Keep in mind that most international restaurants close for several hours between lunch and dinner, and if you show up just before closing time, you may not get served.

Eating Out – Dinner:

- In many countries, it's not uncommon for restaurants to open for dinner at around 8p.m. or later. Keep this in mind if you like to eat dinner early.

Eating In:

- Check out the local supermarkets and farmers' markets. You may be able to come up with some creative meals to eat in your room and save some money.

Eating In – Breakfast:

- Explore the many great local bakeries around the world that offer scrumptious breakfast choices.

Eating In – Lunch:

- Think about one of your old standards: peanut butter. If you like peanut butter, we found it in most countries and it doesn't need to be refrigerated. It became one of our staples along with honey on bread for lunch.

Eating In – Dinner:

- Build a relatively inexpensive and easy meal around rotisserie chickens, which we found to be fairly commonplace.

Drinking:

- As a general rule, steer clear of tap water. Fortunately, we found inexpensive bottled water to be in abundant supply everywhere that we traveled.
- Don't expect to find fresh milk in the refrigerated section of supermarkets. Milk in many countries is usually found packaged for long shelf life in a normal supermarket aisle.

Wines of the World:

- Keep an eye out for a plastic corkscrew. If you enjoy wine like we do, you may find it challenging to retain a corkscrew. Airport security often confiscated ours until we found one that was made entirely of plastic.

Making Conversions

The recurring challenges that international travelers face most are adapting to foreign languages, foreign currencies, and different systems of measurements. Fortunately, most of the world uses the metric system, and you probably have some experience with this already as some American products are labeled in metrics such as a one-liter bottle of soda. So, you only need to become familiar with one set of measurement conversions. That's not the case with languages or currencies. We found that putting a little effort into preparing for these challenges ahead of time went a long way. Here, we provide you with some tips and tools that helped us manage these translations and conversions. While we're on the subject of money, we also provide valuable insights into what the trip actually cost us.

Language Barriers

Entering countries where you don't speak the native language might cause you some anxiety. However, you will be surprised how often at least a little English is spoken. We found that learning just a few key local words goes a long way. We'd heard and read this before. It's so true. People almost always responded positively when we spoke a few words in their language. In France, when we asked people, "Parlez-vous Anglais?" (Do you speak English?), they'd usually respond "No," even though they could. So, we would stumble along with a mix of French and English trying to communicate and then, voilà, they'd start responding with some English. And, in some cases, their English was quite good. We don't think they were being rude. Rather, we suspect that they weren't confident in their English, and they didn't want to embarrass themselves by inferring that they spoke the language fluently.

We developed a list of key words that we would try to make sure we knew the foreign language equivalent of. You can find the appropriate translation using Google Translate or on Wikitravel under the country site. Here is the short list of words that we made a habit of looking up and documenting in a Notes app on our mobile phone:

- Do you speak English?
- Hello
- Goodbye
- Please
- Thank you
- You're welcome
- Yes
- No
- Excuse me
- Where is the toilet?

- 1
- 2
- 100
- 200
- 300
- Coffee
- Tea
- Take away
- Water
- The check, please

Google Translate is great for helping with more complicated translations, but you have to be connected to Wi-Fi or a mobile data network for it to work. Also, the iTranslate app is handy because it not only translates phrases, but it also pronounces them out loud. We used this app a lot to communicate with people in their native language. The downside is again you have to be connected to Wi-Fi or a mobile data network for it to work. A great resource to download and use offline is Wikitravel's common foreign language phrase books, including pronunciations. We saved these to our tablets and referred to them when needed. You can always buy a translation book at a local bookstore, but that is just one more thing you have to carry around.

We expected to find English spoken in the international hotel chains, but we actually found it spoken at every hotel we stayed in. When you aren't staying in a hotel, we recommend checking to make sure that someone speaks English at your accommodation before making a reservation. You can usually figure this out on their website or from reviews on forums such as hostelworld and TripAdvisor.

We were pleasantly surprised that many restaurants had a set of English menus or their main menu provided English subtitles. The downside to this is that these are typically the more "touristy" restaurants, which may not be as good as the restaurant tip you got from a local. Even when there is an English menu, the waiter might not speak English, so learning a few key words and using gestures, body language, and sounds can be helpful ways to successfully communicate with strangers. With each new country, we became a little less anxious than the one before regarding our ability to communicate.

One of the precautions worth taking when staying in a foreign place is to take the address written in the local foreign language with you when roaming around the city. This can be especially helpful when relying on a foreign taxi or tuk-tuk to get you home safely at night. This proved helpful to us on more than one occasion.

Most interactions where we lacked a common language to

communicate in were when we wanted to buy something. In such cases, pointing at things and using fingers to show the quantity desired usually got the job done. A good example of this is when we were in Vienna, Austria. We went shopping in a supermarket for one of our typical smorgasbord dinners. We split up to speed up the shopping. One of Rich's assignments was to select a hard cheese. We prefer goat's and sheep's milk cheeses over cow's milk. The young lady working the counter spoke minimal English. She recommended a cheese to Rich that he suspected was made with cow's milk. When he tried to explain his preferences, she didn't understand him. So, he said "No mooooooo." She cracked a smile, went to her terminal to look up the cheese, turned back to Rich pointing to the cheese she had suggested, and said "Moooooo." Now, we're talking. He replied, "Yes, baa baa." She went back to her terminal to look some cheeses up. She returned with a couple of different types of cheese and said "Baa baa." This was too funny, but it worked and we had our sheep's milk cheese.

It is interesting to note the popularity of American pop culture and music around the world. Just about everywhere we went, we heard familiar songs playing over the loudspeakers. The most popular artist by far was Michael Jackson. He continues to be universally adored for his music. We even saw dueling MJ impersonators performing one evening on the streets of Xi'an, China. Seeing street entertainers was a familiar sight for us, but we never imagined seeing it in China of all places.

American brands such as Coca-Cola, McDonalds, 7-Eleven, and others were ever present and have truly become international brands. We were also pleasantly surprised to see the global popularity of TripAdvisor at various lodging establishments and restaurants. Before the year 2000, TripAdvisor didn't even exist. Now, it's ubiquitous.

Familiarizing yourselves with foreign currencies can be an ongoing challenge. One trick is to try to remember the exchange rate and then do the mental math to convert the price to dollars and cents. If you want to be more precise, you can download the XE app on your mobile phone and/or tablet to consult when in need. Despite these tricks, we still made our share of mental math mistakes and underestimated the cost of some purchases. Since we were traveling with backpacks, we didn't purchase any souvenirs because we had no room to store them. So, our unplanned purchases were usually for food or incidentals. Thus, it wasn't a big deal when we messed up. We usually just laughed at our rusty math skills.

It is important to understand the foreign exchange rate before you arrive so that when you find an ATM, you will know how much foreign currency to withdraw. We were pleased to find that the overwhelming majority of ATMs offered instructions in English as an option. When they didn't, we were able to fumble our way through with some educated guesses on how to respond to the required prompts. In some locations, we withdrew hundreds of thousands of units of the local currency, such as the Indonesian rupiah (IDR) where we received over 12,000 IDRs for one dollar. When we went to a spa in Bali and got a couple's massage, it ended up costing us one million rupiah, which is about $80 US. We referred to this as our million-dollar massage, and Rich claims that it was the best massage that he's ever had. If we hadn't done our homework, we would have had no idea that we should withdraw millions of rupiah from the ATM when we arrived in Bali. Knowing this ahead of time helped us save time, inconvenience, and money in ATM fees.

The value of the dollar against foreign currencies can make

a big difference in how you experience countries. Currency rates can make for an incredibly inexpensive trip or an incredibly expensive one. A strong dollar is good when traveling abroad, and conversely, a weak dollar is not. Interestingly, the dollar can be strong against some currencies while, at the same time, be weak against some others. We learned that currency valuations can fluctuate dramatically over time. A good example of this is that in January of the year of our trip's launch, our good friends Ann and Adam from Australia paid us a visit in the USA and the exchange rates were very favorable to them—they got $1.07 US for each of their Australian dollars. Yet, later in the year, when we visited them in November, the Australian dollar was only worth $0.91 US, which means that we were getting $1.10 Australian for each US dollar. That's a 15 percent swing in the value of the currency in less than a year. In this case, we both benefited. During our trip, we found the best value for the US dollar in Thailand and South Africa, while the most expensive countries were Switzerland and the United Kingdom. As luck would have it, the British pound was hitting five-year highs during our visit. The takeaway here is that foreign exchange rates do matter, and some countries can offer exceptional value over others as a result.

The most difficult country for us to manage money in was Argentina. There were a few reasons for this. Credit cards were not as widely accepted there, especially for lodging, as in other countries. Normally, this would mean that we would just carry more Argentinean pesos on us. However, most Argentinean ATMs would only dispense a maximum of 900 pesos, which at the time was the equivalent of about $150 US. They also tacked on significant fees. Thus, the banks were making out quite well by keeping the maximum withdrawal limit low. Furthermore, our cards could only be used once per day as subsequent withdrawal attempts would be denied, even by different banks than where we'd made the initial withdrawal. Some of our multinight stays required a large cash outlay and multiple visits to the ATM, plus we often needed additional cash for food and other incidentals. We had to pull out our backup ATM card so that we could make two maximum withdrawals a day for a few days in order to meet our cash needs. We weren't thrilled about all of the fees the banks gained at our expense, but we had no choice.

Actually, we did have another choice, but we were too risk-adverse to take advantage of it. It turns out that there was a thriving black market in Argentina that was paying up to ten pesos per US dollar even though the official exchange rate was about six pesos to the dollar at the time. We had plenty of US $100 bills on us in case of emergency that we could have exchanged, but we were afraid of counterfeit Argentinean currency, which we'd read about and felt ill equipped to spot. Near the end of our five-week stay in Argentina, we spoke to a few fellow tourists who were taking advantage of the black market without any counterfeit currency issues. In hindsight, we were too conservative, and we could have saved a lot of money by taking advantage of the black market. This was a case where we didn't do a good enough job of scouting a country before visiting it.

Once or twice a week, we checked our bank and credit card accounts. The bank account was easy as the only real transactions hitting it were our ATM withdrawals and our credit card payments. With the ATM withdrawals, we could see what exchange rate we received, and they were always reasonable. However, we noticed that we weren't getting the foreign bank ATM fees automatically rebated like we should have. That's because they were embedded in the withdrawal amount. So, every few months, we used Skype to call our bank, Capital One, to explain the situation and seek remedy. After some discussion, the bank credited us with the appropriate rebates.

When checking our credit card statement, we were mostly looking to make sure that we recognized the charges and that no suspicious activity was occurring. Our primary credit card was from Chase bank, and we were unable to see the exchange rate until our monthly statement was posted. When the statement came out, we didn't bother to check the exchange rate of each transaction. We looked at a few of them and never saw a problem with them. However, we noticed that some transactions were posted in dollars without an exchange rate. This can happen voluntarily because some payment systems would ask us if we want to pay in US dollars or the local currency. This is a convenient way for payment systems to sneak in a less favorable exchange rate to their benefit and our loss. As a rule, whenever we were asked which currency we wanted to pay in, we always paid in the foreign currency because we knew that Chase would always give us a fair and reasonable exchange rate. So, we became suspicious whenever we saw a charge posted in US dollars with no exchange rate listed.

It turns out that some establishments, without asking our permission, were converting our foreign currency purchases into US dollars at exchange rates that were favorable to them and posting the charge amount in US dollars. In particular, we found most rental car agencies were doing this. Each time that this occurred, we had to dispute the charge and identify the amount that we'd been overcharged. Once we noticed that this was happening, we made sure that we saved each of our rental car receipts to see whether or not we were overcharged. Fortunately, Chase makes it fairly easy to dispute the charge online. We recouped hundreds of dollars that we'd been overcharged this way. In hindsight, we should have saved all of our credit card receipts to ensure that we were charged the correct amount. We suspect that we were overcharged in a few more instances, but we hadn't saved the receipt to verify against. We also received some bogus credit card charges from rental car agencies in Europe that we disputed. They took quite a bit of time and effort on our part before they were resolved to our satisfaction. We're not suggesting that you spend too much time agonizing over foreign transaction fees, but it's a good practice to get in to double check what you're being charged, especially with rental cars.

How Much Is Enough?

By now, you're probably wondering, how much did this trip cost us? We averaged $275 and 6,000 points a day. If you converted the points at a penny a point, then the 6,000 points would be equivalent to $60 per day. Combining the two would come out to $335 per day. In reality, we got a lot more value than a penny a point. We base this on the retail cost of the airfares and rooms we received in return for our points. The Delta Sky Miles example from the "Transportation" chapter is a good illustration of how well we leveraged our points as we received five cents per point. That said, if we hadn't had the points, we would have made more economical choices. In the Delta Sky Miles example, we might have opted for bus travel instead of air travel. We provide this data as a point of reference for you. Our travel blog provides a good sense of how we traveled. We could have done it much cheaper, and we could have lived it up and spent a lot more. In total, we spent about what we thought we would. Perhaps, that's because we had a number in mind and we made choices and tradeoffs that kept us in the ballpark. Of course, we were hoping that we'd spend less and have even more money left over at the end of our trip, but that wasn't to be. In the end, we're happy with the choices that we made, and we definitely feel that we got our money's worth. Here's a little more insight into how we managed our money and points while on the road.

We occasionally checked our joint brokerage account to see how our stock market investment was doing. About once a month, we roughly totaled up our assets (bank and brokerage accounts) and our liabilities (credit card balances) and determined how much money we were spending and how much we had left. This gave us a sense of our monthly expense rate, and then we divided our balance by the monthly rate to see how many more months we could afford to stay on the road. The stock market has its ups and downs, so the runway of months we had left was subject to fluctuation. Luckily, the market and our travel fund investments moved higher while we were away, comfortably extending our runway. Toward the tail end of our trip, we needed to start tapping into our brokerage account. Once a month, we sold just enough stock to cover our projected expenses for the month ahead. This enabled our travel fund investments to continue to grow or decline, according to the whims of the market. However, we still had conviction about our investments, and this was a risk that we were willing to take. We luckily continued to be rewarded.

We also kept track of our various frequent flier and reward point accounts. We tried our best to keep our balances current as we used up our points. This enabled us to know which airlines and/or hotel brands we could still shop for reward travel. Most reward programs would email us monthly account statements. The account balances they provided were usually a week or two old. So, we didn't use them to update our balances. Rather, we used them as a tickler to check the account online and update our balance. Some of our balances actually increased as we traveled because we earned points on them for spending money on our trip.

Managing Your Credit:

It's a good idea to keep an eye on your credit card charges and balances. We had to monitor the balance of our primary credit card to keep an eye on how much credit we had left to spend against. The credit limit on our card of choice (Chase Sapphire) wasn't as high as we would have liked. So, we would sometimes have to pay down our debt before it was due in order to free up some breathing room. We did this rather than use another credit card because we placed such a high value on the Chase Sapphire reward points. The reason for this is that they can be easily transferred to other reward programs without any fee (e.g., United's MileagePlus Program), and we received a 20 percent discount on travel purchases when using our points through Chase.

We also weren't in the best standing with Chase on this account because we carelessly missed one of our first payments on the card. When we set up the card to auto-debit from our bank account, we had fat-fingered the account number and the subsequent transaction failed. We didn't find out about the failure until we got our next statement charging us interest and a late fee. We were able to get Chase to forgive the interest and late fee, but our account was flagged such that we would have to wait an extra fourteen days after we made a payment to ensure that it cleared before Chase would readjust our credit balance. This resulted in our card being rejected late in our billing cycle when we tried to use it, which was both embarrassing and frustrating. So, as soon as we noticed that our credit card payment cleared our bank, we would have to call Chase and have Chase call Capital One while we were still on the line, for a three-way call, to confirm that our payment had indeed cleared so that Chase would lower our credit balance allowing us to continue to use the card. The good news is that after playing this game for six months, our account was placed back in good standing and our credit balance was automatically reset on the date the payment was made. Wouldn't you know it? Shortly after we returned from the trip, Chase raised our credit limit substantially without our asking for it.

The Tax Man

You may leave home for an extended vacation, but you can't escape the tax man. You will, of course, encounter all sorts of taxes on your journey. We just accepted this. Given that we were traveling with backpacks, we weren't making any expensive purchases to bring back home with us. If you plan to make such purchases abroad, you should become familiar with the local tax codes as you may be eligible for a significant rebate of Value Added Tax or VAT as it's more commonly known. Pay close attention to the rules. As we experienced on other trips, unless you follow the rules precisely, you'll forfeit your rebate.

Since we were away for a year, we had to deal with filing our income taxes while we were on the road. We probably could have filed for an extension, but we anticipated a decent refund coming our way and we wanted to add it to our kitty. We prefer paperless delivery to the US Postal Service. So, we received most of what we needed electronically. When going paperless wasn't an option, our mail was rerouted to Elizabeth's parents and they included any tax forms that they received in one of their care packages to us. We sacrificed some privacy by doing this, but we were comfortable doing so. We use TurboTax to self-prepare our income taxes. So, we found a coupon code online and purchased and downloaded a digital version of the software that we needed. Fortunately, we qualified to file both our state and federal taxes electronically, and we arranged to have our refunds direct deposited to our joint bank account. This is where saving a digital image of one of our checks in the cloud came in handy as we were able to readily obtain the bank routing and account numbers from it to enable the direct deposit.

Metric System

Most of the world is on the metric system, but the USA still clings to the imperial system. If you're not used to the metric system, this can add a layer of complexity to your trip. Shopping can get extra complicated because you will first have to convert the currency to understand the cost of the item and then convert the quantity to units you are more familiar with.

In the USA, many liquids in the supermarket are listed in both metric and imperial units. The same holds true for wine and spirits. So, you might have some familiarity with liquid conversions already. Most of the wines of the world are sold in the standard 750-milliliter sizes that we have in the USA making for a seamless transition. However, we did find some places, such as Croatia, where one-liter sizes were more common, and this threw us off a little as we might end up drinking more wine than we'd planned on. Things get a bit more challenging with fuel. The USA sells gasoline in gallons while the rest of the world uses liters. A gallon is approximately equivalent to 4.5 liters. So, you can multiply the liter price by four and then convert the cost to dollars and cents to get a rough idea of the price of a gallon of fuel.

Speed limits are posted in kilometers just about everywhere, except for the US and the UK. If you are driving, you'll be thankful that the speedometers are calibrated in kilometers, so the adjustment isn't a problem. That said, we would never drive over 100 miles per hour back home. So, when our speed was getting up over 100 kilometers, we had to check ourselves and do the mental math to better understand how fast we were going. There are 1.6 kilometers in a mile. Thus, at 100 kilometers per hour, you are traveling at the equivalent of 62 miles per hour. Some of the speed limits can get as high as 130 kilometers per hour or about 81 miles per hour. This is considerably higher than the maximum speed limits that we were used to in the USA. Some of the small cars that we rented were unable to maintain such a speed when we were going uphill.

We found ourselves most challenged with speed conversions when using treadmills. We're used to setting them in miles per hour not kilometers per hour, and we'd also vary our speeds from time to time depending upon how we were feeling that day. Eventually, we figured out our preferred settings in kilometers. The funny thing was that by the time we'd arrived in the UK, where some of the treadmills were calibrated in miles per hour, we had grown accustomed to thinking in kilometers per hour. We inadvertently cranked up the machines to a much higher number associated with kilometers per hour. We couldn't keep pace with the machine and quickly realized our error. Then, we weren't exactly sure of what our normal settings were in miles per hour because we'd forgotten them. So, we had to do some trial and error and mental math to get back on track.

The last main metric conversion we faced is converting pounds to grams or kilograms. We found ourselves somewhat perplexed in the fitness centers where all of the weights are measured in kilograms. This becomes even more challenging because the amount of weight used to exercise various muscle groups varies. Stepping on the scale is a great feeling, though – like you went on a huge diet – because there are 2.2 pounds in a kilogram. So, if you weigh 150 pounds, the scale says you weigh 68.2 kilograms.

Our biggest metric challenge with weight conversions was ordering lunchmeats at the deli counter in a supermarket. People order their lunchmeats in grams. While this shouldn't be too difficult to calculate, the real trouble is communicating that in a foreign language. Sometimes, we weren't even sure what the meat was, but that's another story. To make it easier, we pointed to the meat that we wanted and told the server how many grams we wanted. Usually, we ended up with what we desired.

Key Ingredients

Making Conversions:

Language Barriers:

- Learn a few key words in the local language. Start with our short list of key words and phrases and modify it to fit your needs. Then take a little time to translate your list into the local language before you arrive.
- Grab a business card or have someone write down the address of where you're staying in the local language, just in case you need it to show to a taxi driver to get you back to your lodging.
- Consider downloading and installing the iTranslate app or an equivalent to help you translate foreign languages and hear how words are pronounced.

Foreign Exchange:

- Make a note of the foreign exchange rate for the local currency.
- Calculate the amount of your first ATM withdrawal in foreign currency before you arrive in a new country so that you're prepared for your first withdrawal upon arrival.
- Consider downloading and installing the XE app or an equivalent to help you quickly convert the value of foreign currency into US dollars.
- Keep an eye on your credit card transactions to ensure that you're not being overcharged for currency exchanges. We found that rental car agencies, in particular, would frequently convert our charges to dollars at exchange rates favorable to them but not to us. We had to dispute these charges to get them corrected.

How Much Is Enough:

- Set up a daily budget as a guide to help manage your travel funds.
- Monitor your cash and reward point balances so that you can make informed choices along the way.

Managing Your Credit:

- Keep an eye on your credit balances on your credit cards to prevent having your card rejected.

The Tax Man:

- If you plan to make significant purchases while abroad, familiarize yourselves with the local tax regulations. You may be eligible for a VAT refund that may be significant.
- If you intend to file your income taxes while on the road, be sure to pre-arrange to receive your tax forms electronically wherever possible.

Metric System:

- Familiarize yourself with imperial to metric conversions such as: 1 gallon = 4.5 liters, 1 mile per hour = 1.6 kilometers per hour, and 1 pound = 2.2 kilograms.

Hygiene and Fitness

We all have common personal hygiene needs, and while they're not the most exciting things to talk or write about, they're important. Some of the things that we take for granted when we're in the comforts of our own home can't always be relied upon when traveling. In this section, we shed light on what you can expect in terms of hygiene on the road and provide some tips to help you be prepared for the situations that you may encounter on your journey. If you're into exercising to stay fit, we also share our approach to finding affordable fitness centers.

Bathing

We recommend travelling with small refillable containers of shampoo and conditioner, a bar of soap in a re-sealable plastic bag, and a microfiber towel. This ensures you have the basics covered. Every place where we stayed had at least a shower, and some had bathtubs. On our safari, some of the showers lacked running water and consisted of a metal tank filled with a bucket or two of warm water, but they did the trick as long as we used the water sparingly. Most places provided soap and shampoo and sometimes even hair conditioner. However, you usually get what you pay for, and we found that lower priced accommodations such as hostels offered the least amenities. In some cases, nothing was provided, including towels. In some of these situations, a normal towel could be rented for a reasonable fee. When we knew that the water was unsafe for drinking purposes, we tried to keep this in mind when showering and avoided accidentally ingesting any water. When it came to brushing our teeth in such places, we made a point to use bottled water and always kept a bottle next to the sink as a reminder.

Toiletries

If you are not checking bags, you'll be limited to one quart-sized re-sealable plastic bag for gels and liquids. For the most part, this worked out well for us, and we were usually able to find replacement products with a few exceptions. We did notice some significant variances on what could be found in a supermarket versus a pharmacy. Rich wears contact lenses, and the daily solution he used for these was the item that had to be replaced most often. He found that carrying two four-ounce containers fit in the bag and consistently got through security even though they were over the limit of 3.4 ounces. When it came time to resupply, he occasionally had difficulty finding his preferred brand and had to settle for a substitute until he could locate his brand of choice. In some countries, such as Italy, he had to buy the solution at an optician. While not a gel or liquid, but related nonetheless, over-the-counter pain relievers can vary from country to country. Thus, we learned to stock up on our pain reliever of choice, ibuprofen, and carry it with us. We made sure to fill the empty space of the container with cotton balls or tissues so that the tablets didn't break up as they were bounced around in our backpacks.

There's one subject that's not a lot of fun to talk about, but it is something that's important especially when traveling. And, that is what we commonly refer to in the USA as "going to the bathroom." We had some concern about the condition of public restrooms in other countries. Here's what we found.

The most common terms used abroad for a public restroom are simply a "toilet" in the local language or a "water closet," which is usually abbreviated as plain old "WC." In general, we usually were able to find a public restroom when we needed one. Sometimes, we dropped in on a familiar fast food chain or a restaurant. Once in a while, we had to pay to use a restroom. We carried loose change in our pockets for whenever the need arose. For the most part, our biggest challenges were in Asia. Restrooms weren't always sanitary and often lacked modern toilets, toilet paper, and soap and water to wash our hands. Thus, we learned in Asia to always carry some toilet paper with us. Throughout the trip, we also made a point to carry a small bottle of hand sanitizer.

For whatever it's worth, we were somewhat fascinated by the wide variety of shapes and sizes that toilets themselves actually come in. The most difficult types to adapt to were in China, where the toilet is often not much more than a hole in the floor (for women, you need to get used to squatting). In Osaka, Japan, we encountered one that had a faucet on top of the water tank. When you flushed the toilet, water flowed out of the faucet into the lid of the water tank until it was refilled. Then, there were the water-free bio-models in Uganda, where we had to shovel a few scoops of some granular sand mixture into the unit after each use. The top-of-the-line clearly goes to Japan (outside of the one in Osaka), where most of the toilets were electronic and did things that we didn't dare try. It was tough sometimes just trying to figure out what button to push to get the contraption to flush. We did appreciate the heated seats on some models though. Then there's the bidet, a ceramic unit for washing private parts that was prevalent in most parts of the world but not in the USA.

Just as there seemed to be a never-ending variety of toilets, the same could be said for sinks and faucets. They come in all sorts of shapes and sizes. Regarding the faucets, it would sometimes be a challenge to figure out how to turn the water on. The same could be said for the water controls in showers. Not only was it a challenge figuring out how to turn them on and regulate the temperature, it was often tricky determining how to switch the flow from the tub to the showerhead. Overall, bathrooms often became a source of amusement for us.

Laundry Time

While you can get away with wearing the same clothes over and over, at some point, they're going to need to be washed. Fortunately, most of our clothes were synthetics that lent themselves to hand-washing and air-drying. Every now and then, we got lucky and stayed in a place with a washing machine, which was a real luxury. When this happened, we often washed all of our clothes – a reset of sorts for our wardrobe. The surprising thing was that most of the world gets along just fine without a clothes dryer. We're not opposed to air-drying our clothes, but it takes a long time and it was rare that we'd have a regular clothesline or a rack to hang things on. Thus, a couple of travel clotheslines can come in handy for stringing your clothes out to dry.

Based on some travel sites we scoured, we decided to start out with a Fels-Naptha laundry bar and a couple of elastic clotheslines that Rich's sister, Gwen, had been thoughtful enough to give us before we left. When we ran out of the soap bar, we advanced to powdered laundry detergent. This actually cleaned a little better, but it made a mess when it leaked in one of our backpacks. The most convenient thing that we found was liquid laundry detergent in a tube developed especially for travelers. This worked fine when we were in a country for a long time, but we'd have to get rid of it before every flight since we weren't checking our bags and the tube would be too large to get through airport security.

When the bathroom sink was large enough, we washed our clothes in it in batches. When it was too small, we washed them all together in one big batch in the bathtub, if we had one. Obviously, we had no choice when all we had was a shower stall. We found that the easiest way to rinse clothes was in the shower. After rinsing the clothes twice to ensure that we got all of the soap residue out of them, we wrung the clothes out as best as we could by hand. When we were ambitious, we also rolled the clothes in a towel to try to further remove the moisture from them. After that, we strung out our elastic clotheslines and hung the clothes up. We usually did this in the bathroom as long as we could find things to hook the clotheslines on. Sometimes, we also hung wet clothes on hangers in a closet if we felt the air circulation was good enough for them to dry there.

We tended to wash clothes frequently rather than let the laundry build up. This helped to make the chore less daunting. Aside from the fact that it was boring and time consuming, washing our clothes by hand worked out well for us. We can honestly say that we never had a problem with any sort of odor build up. Then again, who knows, maybe we just got used to the smell, as our clothes probably all smelled the same. No matter, at least, they smelled fine to us.

Exercise

If you are anything like us, you like to eat and drink. Too much of a good thing can catch up with you; so you might want to try to make exercise a priority during your trip. Despite maintaining a fairly regular exercise routine, we each gained about ten pounds on the trip. We were holding our own until we got to Europe and France, in particular. It could have been a lot worse if we hadn't exercised regularly. Fortunately, we were pretty disciplined about exercising before we left for our trip. So, the challenge was not getting lazy while we were on the road. Of course, we did a lot of walking during the trip, sometimes with our backpacks. We also like to hike and got some great workouts on the trails. However, we wanted to do more to try to maintain our weight and fitness. We'll admit that, for whatever reason, we didn't have quite the same focus and intensity during the trip as we did back home. Maybe, it was the lack of stress in our lives that mellowed us a little. Nevertheless, we did our best to find places to get a workout in.

After visiting countries around the world, we really missed how many gyms there are in the US and how easily we could access them. It became a bit of a struggle to find decent gyms around the world. If you're into fitness, select a hotel that has a fitness center. It's convenient and saves the cost of paying for a local fitness center (if you can find one). What some hotels call a fitness center can be a joke, however. We found this out the hard way. One so-called fitness center in Argentina only had four pieces of decrepit equipment, one of which was a vibrating massage lounge chair. So, when you're doing your hotel search, try to look for pictures of the fitness center on the hotel's website. When that doesn't work, try Google "images" searches for gym and the hotel name.

When your accommodation doesn't include a fitness center, look for one in the community where you are staying at a price you are willing to pay. If there was a decent fitness center in the town that advertised its price online, we would try to book a cheaper accommodation and pay the daily fee for the gym. We found that fitness centers/gyms come in all shapes and sizes. Community centers tended to be the largest and often most affordable option for us. The fitness center chains tended to be the most expensive; after all, that's the business that they're in. Offering the most variation, the independent local fitness centers were the most interesting option.

Visiting fitness centers added some intrigue and provided additional perspective about the local culture, at least as it relates to fitness. We also met some interesting characters. As for the costs, they varied dramatically. In some cases, we found free passes online. Since these are intended to attract new customers not tourists, sometimes they were honored and sometimes they were not. The most expensive country was Switzerland, where the going rate at multiple gyms was $35 each per visit. It was as if there was a price-fixing conspiracy going on. This was beyond what we were willing to pay, but we still wanted to work out. So, we put the money toward finding a better accommodation that included a fitness center.

It is worth noting that the operating hours for fitness centers can be unpredictable. On more than one occasion, we were surprised to find the fitness center closed when we'd expected it to be open even in hotels. The most extreme case was in a hotel in Argentina where the small fitness center was only open from 5p.m. to 9p.m. Then, there were places where the gym opened at 7a.m. one weekday and then noon the next one. On the plus side, we found some gyms that were open twenty-four hours a day. The coolest one was in Glasgow, Scotland, where it was all self-serve. We used a kiosk to pay the daily fee, and it issued us a pin code that we then entered on a keypad to gain entry to a spaceship-like pod that ensured that only one person could enter at a time. The pin code was good for twenty-four hours. Thus, we were able to time it so that we got workouts in on back-to-back days for just a single daily fee.

Getting a good workout doesn't mean you have to go to a gym, that is just what we prefer. Running, walking, and hiking around town are excellent ways to see the surroundings and gain a new perspective on where you are visiting. You can also do calisthenics and sit-ups to help keep your muscles toned. To save space and weight in our backpacks, we were both traveling with ultra lightweight running shoes that were not the best for running outdoors. Rich's shoes were so light that he felt like he was running in slippers. Nevertheless, we found it refreshing and fun to run outdoors, and we chalked up some fond memories along the way.

Key Ingredients

Hygiene and Fitness:

Bathing:
- Pack small three-ounce refillable containers of shampoo and conditioner.
- Pack a bar of soap in a resealable plastic bag.

Toiletries:

- Bring along your pain reliever of choice (e.g., ibuprofen) in enough quantity that it'll last you for a while, as you may not be able to find it when you need it.

Taking Care of Business:

- Have on hand some loose change in the local currency in your pocket in case you need to pay to use a public toilet.
- Always keep some toilet paper in your daypack, especially in third world countries.
- Carry a small bottle of hand sanitizer with you throughout the trip.

Laundry Time:

- Pack a couple of travel clotheslines and a bar of laundry soap such as Fels-Naptha (sealed in an airtight plastic bag to help contain the strong perfume).
- Keep an eye out for a tube of travel laundry detergent in the supermarket aisles. This is the most convenient cleaning solution when doing laundry in your bathroom.
- Rinse your clothes in the shower after washing them to get rid of soapy residue.
- Roll your clothes in a towel after wringing them out to soak up excess moisture and help them dry faster.

Exercise:

- If you plan to exercise in a hotel fitness center, be sure to scout out some pictures of it online before booking the hotel so that you're not disappointed by what you find upon arrival.
- Consider using the exercise facilities at a local community center. We usually found them to be the most affordable option when available.

Handling Adversity

The longer that you're away, the more likely it is that you'll encounter some adversity. We all know that this is part of life, whether we're traveling or not. Thus, adversity on the road is nothing new, but being in a foreign land where you're out of your comfort zone can make it a little more challenging to deal with. In this section, we start out with the safety precautions that we took followed by some calculated risks that we took. Then, we move on to share some adversities that we faced and how we dealt with them. We hope you can benefit from our safety precautions and learn from some of our mistakes.

Staying Safe

If you have real concerns about your safety, do your homework before arriving. That means studying the websites of the US State Department, Wikipedia, Fodor's, and Lonely Planet, and skimming travel forums such as TripAdvisor. Many of the common scams, pickpocketing, and crimes of various sorts are the same as what you would perhaps face in many big cities in the USA. As long as you take precautions to minimize risk, you will probably be fine. Fortunately, we didn't run into any serious issues and arrived home safe and sound. Here are the types of precautions that we took and the minor issues we encountered.

We chose not to visit countries where we felt the risks were too high. Usually, this was due to political unrest or terrorist threats. We considered the information on the US Department of State's website, and we also paid attention to what was going on in the international news from sources like CNN.com's international site. As a result, we skipped countries like Kenya, Egypt, and Greece. Why Greece you might wonder? The Department of State's Safety and Security section started out as follows: "The US government remains deeply concerned about the heightened threat of terrorist attacks against US citizens and interests abroad." This didn't give us a warm and fuzzy feeling. When we combined this information with the fact that unemployment in Greece was over 25 percent, we were concerned that this could lead to a higher risk of crime. We'd still like to visit Greece someday, but we prefer to do it when we feel that it's safer.

We also skipped countries based on word-of-mouth warnings from friends, families, and other travelers. Therefore, we skipped Brazil. We heard just too many negative crime-related experiences for our liking, and we had other countries that we were more interested in seeing in South America. We're not suggesting that you skip these countries just because we did; we know people who have had wonderful experiences in each of them. Rather, we're suggesting that you do your own research on *any country* before you travel to get the most current information and make your own informed decisions based on what you learn and feel about a country.

The number one tip for staying safe once inside a country is to be aware and pay attention, especially when in crowded places such as street markets, train stations, subways, etc. Rich kept his wallet, passports, and cash in zippered pockets. He placed his camera in one front pocket and his mobile phone in the other. In crowded conditions, he tried to keep his hands on his front pockets to better protect these items. Elizabeth had a single strap crossover shoulder bag in which she kept her wallet and cash. She was able to keep a close hold of this bag and never had an issue. Neither of us wore expensive or flashy jewelry. By taking these precautions, we made ourselves less appealing and more difficult targets for pickpockets and petty thieves. We observed numerous tourists who would be much easier targets for thieves to prey on. As an example, we often saw tourists walking along with big expensive-looking cameras casually held in one hand by their side. That being said, we're happy to report that we did not witness any crimes taking place during our trip.

When we had a safe in our room, we secured our passports, backup credit/debit cards, extra currency, laptop, and other devices in it. When we didn't have a safe, we locked these items in our backpacks in our room. When we were in between lodging locations and had a rental car, we rarely left our backpacks in the trunk of the car. We always tried to make a point to check in to our next accommodation and store our bags in our room. The good news is that none of the cars that we rented were ever broken into, but if they had been, the thief wouldn't have found anything of real value. We had small combination Master locks on our backpacks. We realize that a thief could have sliced the bags open with a sharp knife. The locks were more of a deterrent to prevent any dishonest hotel staff from going through our things. On a few occasions, we stored our bags for a few hours in a hotel storage room. We felt a little more exposed when we did this, and that's why we didn't make a habit of it.

With few exceptions, we did not stay out late at night. Since we followed the warm weather, the daylight hours were long in most places. Therefore, even when we went out to dinner in the evening, we often were back in our room before dark. When we did venture out late at night, we inquired about the safety of the area with the local staff before we did. When we were in Logroño, Spain, we were out late on several nights partaking in some tapas crawls. We had heard that the area we were staying in was quite safe to walk at night. So, we walked back to our hotel and did so without incident. That's not to say that this was the wisest thing to do. It probably wasn't, but if we were going to go barhopping late at night, this was a better place to do it than most.

While we didn't run into any major safety issues, we did have a few minor ones. The first one occurred in Buenos Aires, Argentina. We usually tried to schedule our flights so that we would arrive in the middle of the day. It was just another small safety precaution. On this occasion, our flight didn't land until 10:30p.m. Our pre-arrival scouting informed us that the best mode of transportation into the heart of the city, where we were staying, was to take a taxi, which should cost about 250 pesos plus tolls. We had read warnings not to take a curbside taxi; rather, the safer choice was to pre-pay for a taxi at a booth inside the airport terminal. When we arrived at the booth, we found that the wait time would be thirty to forty-five minutes. We were tired and our usual, impatient selves. Elizabeth speaks some Spanish. So, despite the warnings, we decided to try hailing a curbside taxi.

We had to compete with other travelers trying to do the same thing, so taxis were scarce on this particular night. Luckily, we scored one after about ten minutes, but the driver wanted 320 pesos including tolls. We tried negotiating a lower fare, but he wouldn't budge and we reluctantly agreed. The driver made small talk and seemed friendly enough on the way in. Rather than pull into the hotel's circular entrance driveway, he pulled over to the side of the street opposite the hotel, which seemed a little unusual. While it's unnecessary to tip taxi drivers in Buenos Aires, the guy seemed nice enough and it was late at night. So Rich gave him an extra 20 pesos making it 340 pesos, which at the time was the equivalent of about $50. The driver took the money, counted it, then turned around holding 70 pesos and accused Rich in Spanish of shortchanging him. Not understanding Spanish, Rich was puzzled by the driver's reaction. Elizabeth had to intervene to interpret. Since she hadn't handled the money, she assumed that the driver was honest and that Rich had made a mistake with the new currency. But Rich held his ground, confident that he had indeed given the driver the correct amount. The driver started getting loud and became adamant that he'd been shortchanged. Now it was Rich's turn to get angry; he started accusing the driver of being a crook. As Rich got louder, the driver started to back off.

We got out of the car with our backpacks, and the driver quickly sped off. Elizabeth turned to Rich and asked how he was so sure that he was right and the driver was wrong. It was simple, he replied, the first thing we usually do when we arrive in a country is go to the ATM to withdraw cash in the local currency. The ATM dispensed mostly crisp new 100 peso bills. Rich had paid the driver with three of these crisp new bills and two twenty peso bills. The driver had performed a quick slight-of-hand replacing the three 100 peso bills with three ten peso bills. Had we fallen for this deception, we would have been out another 270 pesos or more than $40. And to think that we tipped this guy and he still tried to rip us off. We learned a couple of valuable lessons from this. First, pay attention to cash paid and change received, if any, in all transactions because shortchanging unwary customers is a common scam. Second, we need to heed the advice we receive. In this case, we should have avoided the curbside taxis.

We had a few other issues with taxi drivers who tried to overcharge us. We took a metered taxi from our hotel in Bangkok, Thailand, to the airport. When the taxi driver didn't start the meter as we left the hotel, we asked him to turn it on. He argued with us for a while and then reluctantly turned the meter on. Throughout the ride to the airport, he tried to convince us that we should be paying a flat rate that we knew would be much higher than the metered rate. Fortunately, we had checked with the hotel's doorman on what the taxi fare should be before we left, and we knew that the drivers should be using the meter and what the approximate cost would be. It wasn't the most pleasant taxi ride we've ever had but, at least, we didn't overpay for it.

In Agra, India, we arranged for a bicycle rickshaw to take us from the Taj Mahal ticket booth to the entrance gate, which was about one kilometer away. The driver was to wait for us and then take us back to the ticket booth, which he did. He then proceeded to try to charge us double the price that we had pre-arranged, which we almost fell for. In both cases, we tipped the drivers a fair amount, despite our frustration. After all, at the end of the day, they're just trying to make a living.

We also fell victim to a "bait and switch" scam in Morocco when we overpaid for a local SIM card for our mobile phone at an airport kiosk. Normally, we buy our SIM cards from the telecommunications company itself rather than a third party, but there were none to be found at the airport terminal in Casablanca where we arrived. So, we settled for a small third party kiosk advertising SIM cards. The man behind the counter spoke enough English for us to communicate what we needed, and he quoted us a price of $20. We agreed to the purchase under the condition that he install the card and get it operational for us, which he did. However, when he rang up the bill, it was $45 instead of the $20 price he'd quoted us. When we mildly protested, he explained that the SIM card was indeed $20, but the voice, text, and data service accounted for the additional $25. Given the language barrier and our fatigue after a long day of travel that started at 2:30a.m. in Uganda with a transfer in Cairo, we decided to just accept it and move on. We learned another lesson. Just stick to dealing with the mobile carriers themselves, and that's what we did for the rest of the trip.

We suspect that we probably, unknowingly, got scammed a few more times along the way, but this was the only time that it became obvious. We read about lots of scams; thus, we had our antennae up and steered clear of them. One common scam is where the tuk-tuk driver makes an unplanned stop at a jewelry store. If you're unfamiliar with the term tuk-tuk, it's a three-wheeled, open-air taxi found throughout much of Asia. There are quite a few variations of them. When our tuk-tuk driver in Phuket, Thailand, informed us that he was going to make such a stop, we pleaded with him to keep going. He then let us in on a little secret. The jewelry store gave him a free liter of gasoline for every customer that he brought into the store, whether the customer made a purchase or not. So, we relented. It was a really hot day, and it turned out that the jewelry store was air-conditioned. We browsed the overpriced goods in the extensive store while we cooled off. We then left without making a purchase. The staff in the store weren't too happy with us, but our driver sure was.

Some say that the real joy of travel is in retrospect after you return from the trip. There is some truth to that, but you probably want to enjoy your trip while you are on it, not just after it is over. Thus, you might be somewhat hesitant to venture outside of your comfort zones, but if you do, challenging yourselves and overcoming some fears can truly reward you. For us, this led us to some extraordinary experiences that greatly enhanced our trip. It also led us to one experience that we have no intention of ever repeating.

This may sound a bit contradictory coming off the heels of a section on minimizing risk. However, we want to share with you a few stories so you can see what we mean. We were really on the fence about whether to visit Thailand or not. On the one hand, it held an exotic appeal for us, while on the other hand, it had a history of political unrest and we'd read about more scams going on in Thailand than anyplace else that we planned to visit. It is probably fair to say that we were intimidated by the prospect of visiting Thailand. Yet, we were trying to keep an open mind. On a group tour of Taroko National Park in Taiwan, where, by the way, we experienced a minor earthquake, a fellow American named Julie Johnson told us about Phuket, Thailand. Julie raved about the sea caves kayaking trip that she took to James Bond Island. After chatting with her and looking at the amazing pictures and videos on her iPad, we were won over. This turned the tide, and we decided that evening that we would visit Thailand. We were now excited about Phuket but still somewhat wary of Bangkok. We had to fly into Bangkok. So, we decided to stay there for just two nights. We wish it had been longer. We really enjoyed Bangkok, Phuket, and Chiang Mai. In fact, Thailand was one of the top highlights of our trip. If we had let our fears get the best of us, we would have missed out on it.

Rich had been to India several times for business, but Elizabeth had never been there. India is a place that's far outside the comfort zone for most Americans. Yet, it's a place that everyone should get the opportunity to experience at least once in his or her lifetime. Elizabeth was somewhat reluctant to visit based upon the graphic descriptions that Rich had previously shared. Yet, somehow Rich persuaded her to venture there to see the Taj Mahal. As with most first-time visitors to India, it was sensory overload. While Elizabeth is not sure that she wants to return to India, she is glad that she made the trip. The Taj Mahal was exquisite, and she's grateful to have an appreciation for what India is all about. India is a good example of a place, at least for us, that you enjoy more in retrospect than when you are there.

We'd never been to Africa, and when we discussed the continent with friends and family, everyone told us that we had to go on a safari. While the thought of seeing wild animals roaming free sounded thrilling, we are not huge fans of roughing it and sleeping in tents. Many of the people recommending a safari had done just that, and it didn't sound appealing to us. Rich, in particular, was indifferent about going on a safari. This time, it was Elizabeth who convinced Rich to give it a try. As we talked more and more about it, we decided that if we were going to do a safari, it would be really cool if we could see some gorillas in the wild. Our research uncovered that there are only three countries where you can see mountain gorillas in the wild: The Congo, Rwanda, and Uganda. At present, The Congo is not a safe place to visit. Of the remaining two countries, Uganda offered the most diversity for a safari. After more research on tour operators and itineraries, we chose the itinerary and pricing offered by African

Big Five Safaris (www.africanbigfivesafaris.com), but we were having difficulty finding reviews on the Internet. We reached out to the company directly, and a representative provided us with a short list of references from around the world. We contacted each of the references via email and received glowing reviews from all of them. Thus, we ended up booking a ten-day safari with African Big Five.

This was the biggest single expenditure of our trip, but it was well worth it. We had the time of our lives. The tour operator offered an option on the first day to go whitewater rafting on the Nile River. We had a blast. The rapids are world class, and we shared a raft with people from around the world. The wildlife we saw was amazing. We went mountain gorilla trekking and were able to get closer to the family of gorillas than we ever imagined would be possible. We also had the opportunity to visit a remote school and donate supplies where they had so little. We were truly touched by this visit. This was another extraordinary experience that we would have missed, if we hadn't left our comfort zones.

Queenstown in New Zealand is not only one of the most beautiful places in the world, it also bills itself as the adventure capital of the world, offering nearly every conceivable adrenaline-rush sport there is. The first time we were there a few years earlier, Elizabeth persuaded Rich to go skydiving, even though she's afraid of heights. To say that the experience was spectacular would be an understatement. On this trip, we stopped in Queenstown for an afternoon coffee break on our way to the world famous Milford Sound fjords (we'd regrettably missed them on our first visit to New Zealand). Later that evening, we went for a long hike along Lake Te Anau, where we were spending the night. Rich shared with Elizabeth that he'd been thinking all afternoon about Queenstown and bungy jumping. The thought had been rekindled when we drove past AJ Hackett's Kawarau Bridge Bungy Jumping, where we had watched others jump during our first visit but lacked the desire or perhaps the courage to attempt it ourselves. We'd also said then that, if we were ever going to do it, this would be the place. It's the site where commercial bungy jumping originated. The location is stunning, and the height is less intimidating than some of the other sites we've seen. As we hiked further, we discussed the magnetic pull of Queenstown and decided to spend a few days there. We put bungy jumping on the menu but didn't make a decision on it.

When we returned to Queenstown, the young, unassuming hostess who checked us in at the hotel relayed to us how she'd just bungy-jumped five times on her day off earlier in the week. We asked ourselves: Was this a sign? How could we not find the nerve to jump just once if she did five in a day? When we settled into our room, we did a little quick research and learned that this month was the twenty-fifth anniversary of bungy jumping off the Kawarau Bridge. Hmmm, these folks at AJ Hackett obviously know what they're doing if they've been in operation for that long. Then, we discovered that Kawarau Bridge is one of the few places that offers "tandem" jumps. This would allow us to take the plunge together, which was rather appealing. So, sweaty palms, pounding hearts, and all, we set out that very same afternoon. We confronted our fears and somehow found the courage to take the plunge. We're not going to say that it was easy or fun; it was scary as hell. But, it was exhilarating to overcome our fears and have this amazing memory to treasure forever. The people running the operation were fantastic. They even offered us a really deep discount to do it again, but once was enough for us. We gladly checked that one off the bucket list, thank you!

Unfortunately, over the course of your trip, something is probably not going to go the way you want. You may lose something, miss a flight or in our case get deported. In the overall scheme of things, our trip went really well for us. With that said, we had our share of challenges and setbacks. We tried not to let them get the best of us and tried to use ingenuity where we could to improve the situation. Since we travelled with a menu approach, we didn't have a firm schedule. This enabled us to quickly overcome most setbacks. Still, that is not to say that we weren't pretty bummed when they happened.

Losing Stuff: If you've seen our packing list, you know we didn't travel with much. So, when we left something behind, despite what we thought were our best efforts to make sure that we didn't, it was a big deal. Usually, we would realize we left an item after we arrived at our next destination and went to use it. Invariably, it was impractical to return to retrieve the item or items. The problem was that every place we stayed in had a different configuration, and even though we thought we had checked everything, we would miss something. Another problem was that we sometimes incorrectly assumed that the other one of us had already double-checked everything.

The first time we lost something, we were in Japan. Rich realized that he'd left his replacement contact lenses at the hostel near Mount Aso. He was keeping them in a hard case intended for sunglasses. He'd placed it on the bed while rearranging his backpack, and it got lost among the covers. We had moved on to Osaka, which was about four hours away by high-speed train, and we didn't want to lose the time that it would take to go back. We called the hostel, which was gracious enough to ship the contact lenses to the B&B we planned to stay at in Chiang Mai, Thailand. We gave our credit card number and were charged a fair price for the shipping and handling. This was a little risky, but we felt it was worth the risk to get the contacts back. Fortunately, everything worked out and Rich recovered his lenses. You would think that after that incident we'd have learned our lesson, but we continued to leave various articles of clothing and toiletries behind.

In Ubud, Bali, our B&B lacked a closet; it provided an armoire instead. Upon leaving, we didn't think to check the armoire where Rich had hung up his shirt and pants the night before. We'd just bought the polo shirt a few days before in Singapore to add some variety to his limited wardrobe. Well, at least he got to wear it once. The pants were his favorites from ExOfficio, not a brand that we could find in stores where we were headed. This left him with only one pair of convertible pants. He gave up on the idea of adding another shirt but couldn't live without the pants. So, he ordered a pair online and shipped them to Elizabeth's parents to include in the next care package. As the trip continued on, we came to laugh at our stupidity for leaving something behind yet again. All we can say is that when you stay in more than one hundred different places over the course of a year, you need to become as ritualistic as possible when it comes to unpacking and repacking your things, if you want to minimize leaving belongings behind. As far as we're concerned, we still haven't learned our lesson—we left the power adapters for our notebooks behind in a hotel room while traveling within the USA shortly after returning from our trip. This mistake cost us about $200 to replace them and to have the hotel ship the originals to Elizabeth's parents. Oh well, at least, we now have a backup set.

Here are some things we could have done to help combat this problem that you may consider:

1. Make up a checklist of all your belongings and go through it before you leave your room.

2. Check all drawers, closets, and nooks and crannies.

3. Keep your backpack/suitcase organized and put things in the same places over and over so that you can more easily spot if they're missing.

Flight Troubles: There are different rules of thumb for how early to arrive at the airport. Some say two hours for domestic travel and three hours for international travel. What we learned is that every airport, country, and airline is different. So, look online at the boarding process for your air carrier and follow its guidelines. You can use the extra time spent hanging out in the airport for travel planning or reading. When you arrive at the airport, scout out the nearest electrical outlets so that in the event of a delay, you can keep powered up while you wait.

Throughout our trip, we were being extra cautious when it came to getting to the airport in time for our next flight. The primary reason for this was that we were usually unfamiliar with either the airport or the airline and some of the airlines had strict check-in requirements. One airline, Indigo Air, which we flew from Bangkok to Delhi, required us to check in at the airport at least 1.5 hours before departure. It didn't allow us to check in online, and this flight was a connection where we were flying a different airline for the first leg. So, we had to make sure that we booked the first flight such that we'd have enough time to still check in when we arrived in Bangkok. EasyJet requires passengers to be at the departure gate at least thirty minutes prior to departure or forfeit your seat. China Eastern reserved the right to close boarding forty-five minutes before departure.

When it came time to fly to Croatia, we were flying from Paris Beauvais Airport on Ryanair. We had used this airport and airline previously to make a side-trip from France to Spain and had about an hour and a half to kill at the airport. The airports used by the budget airlines, like Ryanair, are almost never conveniently located to the major cities they fly into. Paris Beauvais is no exception. It is approximately ninety kilometers north of Paris. Ryanair recommends purchasing seats on one of its shuttle buses from Paris three hours before your flight's departure time. Since we had plenty of time to spare the first time we flew out of Beauvais, Rich persuaded Elizabeth to cut it closer this time by leaving Paris only two hours before the flight. As you might have guessed, this did not turn out well.

The bus left later than expected and then took longer than expected to get to the airport, leaving us only thirty minutes to get our boarding passes validated at the airline's check-in counter (a requirement for non-EU citizens, like us), clear security, and then clear immigration. Unlike the first time, when the airport was fairly quiet, this time it was mobbed with long lines for check-in and even longer ones for security. Our situation looked hopeless until Elizabeth took charge and saved the day. Displaying no inhibitions, she led the way and pleaded with other travelers to allow us to cut the lines at the check-in counter, security gate, and immigration control. We were the last people to board the plane and made the flight just in the nick of time. Needless to say, we were pretty stressed out because we didn't have a backup plan if we had missed our flight and it was the only one of the day to Croatia. We relearned the lesson that it is better to play it safe and always arrive early at the airport, which you can be sure is exactly what we did for the rest of the trip.

If you do have the misfortune of missing a flight or having one get cancelled, it does no good to dwell on the misfortune. Instead, use it as an opportunity to figure out a creative backup plan. Of course, this is more easily done when you don't have future hotel bookings or activities that you've pre-paid. If you have a flexible travel schedule, look at what other flights are available that day and see if you can get rebooked somewhere else that you'd like to go. Or, see if you can arrive at your destination later than planned by connecting through one of the airline's major hubs. If you can't find a flight, then try to find a nearby hotel with decent Wi-Fi and a free airport shuttle and then use the Internet once you check in to explore your options. Situations like this are certainly stressful, but they can also become somewhat exciting and fun and potentially may lead to an alternate destination that you wouldn't have experienced otherwise.

Don't Get Deported Like We Did: So, this is the embarrassing section where we tell you how we screwed up big time. We talked about visas in the "Appetizer" section, and we're revisiting the topic to show you how to find "loopholes" to the rules and also what happens when you don't follow the rules. Rich was diligent about looking up the visa requirements for each country we visited, so we never anticipated having any issues. But alas, with less than a month left in our trip, our utilization of a "loophole" in the visa regulations of one country exposed us to an overlooked visa regulation of another country, ultimately resulting in our deportation. Here's what happened.

We made plans to visit Helsinki for a long weekend because the flight from Switzerland was cheap and we'd never been to Finland. While Elizabeth was looking over TripAdvisor forums about things to do in Finland, she found people talking about going to Russia visa-free. We hadn't planned to visit Russia because obtaining a Russian visa is a hassle due to the paperwork requirements and it's a bit pricey as well. A Russian visa also requires you to part with your passport for a week or so while it's being processed. As a result, obtaining a Russian visa while we were bouncing around the world was going to be a difficult problem to solve. Once we were on the trip, political tensions arose between the USA and Russia, and we were thinking that given the hassle of obtaining a visa, we'd just drop it from the menu.

When Elizabeth researched the visa-free loophole further, she found that tourists who visit Russia on a cruise could get around the visa requirement as long as their visit is less than seventy-two hours. Great news. The loophole might enable us to see Saint Petersburg without the hassle and cost of obtaining a Russian visa. However, as we've previously shared, cruising is not really our thing, and what are the odds that we could find a short cruise that would fit our schedule in the short time that we had left? That didn't deter Elizabeth. She kept searching and, lo and behold, she found a five-day cruise from Helsinki to Saint Petersburg that would fit both our schedule and our budget. And, we'd only be on the ship two nights (going and returning). The remaining two nights would be in a hotel in Saint Petersburg. This sounded pretty good. So, we booked the trip and got to see the beautiful city that is the setting for many Russian classic books that we love.

The unintended consequence is that taking this cruise exposed us to the Finnish immigration process, which ultimately cut our trip to mainland Europe short and got us deported. When we landed in Helsinki, we took a bus and then a tram from the airport to the seaport where we would embark upon a ship for the overnight cruise to Saint Petersburg. Since we were leaving Finland, we had to go through the immigration exit process. When the young border guard asked us when we'd entered the Schengen Area, we were unprepared with an answer. What's the Schengen Area, you ask? In a nutshell, there's an agreement that creates a borderless area within Europe that permits the free movement of persons among the twenty-six countries participating in the agreement. Tourists like us can enter this area as a whole for pleasure without the need to apply for a visa for a maximum of ninety days in any 180-day period.

He asked us if we understood the Schengen Agreement. We replied that we thought we did; as we understood it, we could only stay within the Schengen Area for ninety days. However, if we left the area and returned, the ninety days would start over again. Well, we were wrong. We were taken out of the line and led away by two armed border guards to the Finnish Border Guard offices, where we were placed on a detention bench and instructed to wait there. After about fifteen minutes, one of the guards came out and in a formal tone said: "The Schengen Agreement provides that tourists may stay in the area for up to ninety days during the preceding 180-day period. We have reviewed your passports, and you have been in the area 112 of the past 180 days. This is twenty-two days over the limit. This means that we're going to have to fine you and deport you."

We said that we accept that we were wrong, but that we didn't intentionally break the rules. Is there any opportunity for leniency as the spirit of the agreement is probably intended to prevent foreigners from entering the area and working, thereby taking jobs away from the local citizens? This got them thinking and the guards disappeared back into their office.

When they came back out they offered to let us take our cruise to Russia, which is not a member of the Schengen Agreement, as long as we didn't come back. If we didn't return on the ship to Helsinki but tried to leave by another form of transportation, we were afraid that we'd run into problems with Russian immigration. Russia is not a place where we wanted to be detained for breaking the law. However, this new option gave us an idea.

We asked, "What if we take the cruise to Saint Petersburg and book a flight at our expense upon our return to a destination outside of the Schengen Area? Would that be possible?" The guards returned to the office to confer again.

We won't bore you with any more of the he-said, she-said drama. Here's what ended up happening. The two more empathetic guards convinced the overzealous guard to let us take the cruise to Saint Petersburg and then deport us upon our return provided that we paid for the airfare. Better yet, there would be no additional monetary fines, as they recognized that we would incur the cost of the airfare and lose a significant amount of money on the airfares that we had already pre-paid but would now be forfeited.

We accepted the terms and were released in time to still make our cruise. While in Russia, we booked a flight from Helsinki to London on the day that our cruise returned; the United Kingdom doesn't participate in the Schengen Agreement. When we returned a few days later, we were pulled out of line by a uniformed border guard who asked us to come with him and he escorted us back into the detention center.

We were detained for approximately four hours while the necessary paperwork was completed. We were served with official deportation documents that we had to sign. Once the formalities were taken care of, the first two border guards who originally detained us escorted us to an official van and drove us directly to the airport. They brought us to the head of the security line and then the head of the immigration line. Once our passports were stamped and we passed through immigration, we were now considered to no longer be in the Schengen Area. We were free to do as we pleased inside the international departures terminal until our flight departed later that afternoon. It felt good to have our freedom back again, even if we had several hours to kill before our flight departed. We are grateful that throughout the whole rather stressful process we were always treated with respect.

Being detained and deported was a frustrating experience and a costly mistake. It cost us about $1,500 in unanticipated airfares and airfares forfeited. However, we learned a valuable lesson: When traveling abroad, you need to pay close attention to the visa requirements of every country that you visit. Our experience also reinforced the need to maintain composure when faced with adversity. Had we let our emotions get the best of us and become angry with the border guards for detaining us when we felt they should have turned a blind eye, we probably would have been immediately deported back to the USA and lost the opportunity to see Saint Petersburg, not to mention the money that we had already paid for the trip. On the bright side, we subsequently got to spend ten unplanned days in the UK and saw a lot of the English countryside that we'd never seen before.

When faced with travel problems, don't just give up like we almost did. Hang in there and try to be creative. You just might find another solution to the problem.

Handling Adversity:

Staying Safe:

- Do your homework before entering a new country. Research safety concerns on websites such as the US State Department, Wikipedia, Fodor's, and Lonely Planet, and skim travel forums like TripAdvisor.
- Avoid countries where you deem the safety risks to be too high. Perhaps, you'll be able to visit sometime in the future when things are safer.
- Heed the safety advice and warnings of experienced travelers to the areas that you're planning to visit.
- There are lots of scam artists who prey on tourists like you. Try to learn about common scams in places that you'll be traveling to so that you reduce the risk of being taken advantage of.
- Be aware of your surroundings and belongings. Keep your cash in a money belt, if possible. Keep your wallet in a zippered front pocket.
- Protect your passports, camera, mobile phone, and tablet when not in use.
- Consider a crossover shoulder strap bag instead of a purse to store your valuables.
- Take advantage of in-room safes, when available, to store all of your valuables when you're not in the room.
- Use a travel combination lock to lock your backpack or suitcase as a theft deterrent.
- Avoid being out late at night when possible.

Overcoming your Fears:

- Keep an open mind and reach outside of your comfort zone every now and then. You just might be rewarded beyond belief.

When Things Don't Go as Planned:

- Make a checklist of things to review before you leave your lodging and routinely review it before leaving. You'll minimize your losses.

- Scan all drawers, closets, and nooks and crannies.
- Keep your backpack/suitcase organized and store items in the same places over and over. That makes it easier to spot when something is missing.
- When flying, make sure that you understand the timelines for checking in and being at the gate so that you don't miss your flight. Be sure to give yourselves some extra cushion.
- Make sure you understand and adhere to each country's visa rules and regulations.
- When adversity strikes, put your heads together and use your ingenuity. You just might surprise yourselves with how things turn out.

Staying Sane and Getting Along

There are a lot of things that might not go the way you intended, which can cause tension between you and your partner throughout your travels. That's why staying sane and getting along is so important. You are going to have a lot of one-on-one time, so before you head out on your trip, you'll want to give some thought to how you're going to entertain yourselves during your free time. It's also helpful to think about how you might document your trip so that you can relive and savor your experiences once again after you return. There are many ways to keep in touch with friends and family, and you should consider just how connected you want to be before you leave so that you have your forms of communications well established. You're probably going to be spending more time together than ever before. So, we relay what it felt like for us as a couple and how we kept our relationship in balance. We also got homesick from time to time. What will you do when these emotions grab hold of you? We describe our approaches on staying sane and getting along on long trips here.

Entertainment

If you plan to be spontaneous in your itinerary during your trip, you will certainly keep yourselves entertained with surfing the Net for travel options. Our tablets made for excellent eReaders, and we each made sure that we had multiple titles downloaded so that we always had something new to read. A voracious reader, Elizabeth put her mom's library card to good use, borrowing digital copies of books, which saved us a lot of money.

Slow Wi-Fi connections can take the fun out of Internet browsing and sometimes you might want something other than a book to keep you entertained. When you turn on the local TV, English programs, if any, are usually going to be limited to CNN and/or BBC news, if that at all. We weren't big TV watchers back home, but we would occasionally get hooked on a TV series, buy seasons of it, and then binge-watch it.

Services like Netflix and Hulu are great if you have high-speed Internet access and can get around the firewalls in certain countries to stream shows and movies. Rather than relying on those services, we recommend you look into purchasing a TV series or two and download the episodes either ahead of your trip or during a time when you have great Wi-Fi. The beauty of downloading media to your notebook is that you don't need an Internet connection to watch an episode.

It gets expensive buying full seasons of a TV series so at times when you have good Internet and are looking to settle into bed with a good show, Netflix is a great money-saving option. At the time, a monthly subscription cost just $6.99, and the service had a lot of good options for TV shows and movies to stream. A problem we ran into with Netflix was that it isn't offered in many of the countries we were visiting. But you can get around this by using VpnOneClick, a subscription VPN service. By logging on to the service, you can change your IP address to the USA or Canada, and circumvent firewalls that wouldn't allow you to log in with a foreign

IP address. While this worked for us, be aware that there's additional Internet bandwidth required to run a VPN connection, so you need a decent Wi-Fi connection to use it. Although we had our share of frustrations with connectivity in different locations, we were able to watch several programs through Netflix and saved some money in the process.

When it comes to movies, we suggest renting rather than buying them. The way this works, if you're not familiar with it, is that you pay a modest fee for the right to watch the movie once. We usually had thirty days to watch the movie from the time that we downloaded it, but once we started to watch it, we only had twenty-four hours to finish it. This arrangement, which we used through iTunes, worked out just fine; it allowed us to download a few movies and then watch them when we were in the mood. As an example, we took advantage of this service to download and watch *Saving Private Ryan* just prior to our visit to Normandy.

For the most part, we downloaded content to our notebook. It had a thirteen-inch diagonal widescreen, which was large enough to enjoy the shows. It's worth noting that High Definition (HD) is usually the default format for downloading. Not only does HD take up more disk space, it tends to cost more. While our notebook can play an HD video, it doesn't have a true HD screen. So, paying for HD made no sense because it would cost more, take longer to download, and take up more space, but because of the resolution on our display, we wouldn't get the benefit of the higher picture quality. Therefore, we always made sure that we selected the Standard Definition (SD) option, when available, and we were more than satisfied with the picture quality. On a few occasions, we also downloaded content to one of our tablets. We did this when we might want to watch a movie in transit on a plane, train, or bus. While less than ideal—the screen was smaller and we had to share a pair of earbuds with each of us getting one bud to listen to—it kept us entertained and helped to pass the travel time.

We also like to listen to music and would often have it playing in the background while we were working on the blog or surfing the Internet. Our primary source of music was our iTunes library, which we played off of the notebook. We were also fond of an app called 8 Tracks that we used to stream music off of the Internet from our mobile phone or tablet. We liked using its search capability to find music with a local flair to complement our state of mind, such as Zen Buddha music when we were in Asia. Thanks goes to our good friend Adam in Australia, who originally introduced us to this fun app. We also had our iPods loaded with music, podcasts, and audiobooks to entertain us while we were working out or in transit.

Preserving Memories

There are so many places these days to share your photos and experiences with friends and family. You can make posts to Facebook, Instagram, and Twitter; upload photo albums to services like Google Photos and Kodak; or create a blog to write about your experiences. We love to travel, but the same couldn't be said for taking pictures. We certainly took pictures wherever we went but not a lot of them. Maybe it's because Rich's dad was a professional photographer, and Rich felt there was no way that he could compete with his dad's work. However, this trip was different. We wanted to memorialize it, so to speak. How many times are you going to take a year off to travel around the world?

So, we decided that we would photograph and document

our trip. Elizabeth had developed know-how when writing a blog to chronicle her experiences overseas while pursuing her graduate studies in Ireland. We decided to leverage that experience and use a blog to document and share our travels. When we finished each post, we uploaded a link to Facebook so our friends and family knew it was available. In time, we were inspired to add some video to spice up our blog. We won't kid you, working on the blog was a time-consuming activity. However, it became a labor of love, and it helped to keep our skills sharp. If you're unfamiliar with blogging, there are many sites available that make it easy. We recommend looking into WordPress, Weebly, and Blogger and seeing which makes the most sense for you.

Here is how we preserved memories and wrote our blog. We started off the trip with just our smartphones as our digital cameras. We made this decision not because we thought they were the best cameras, but because not bringing a digital camera meant one less thing that we needed to tote around the world. Our phones were capable of taking both still pictures and videos. Once in a while, the picture quality would be exceptional, but most of the time, it was just okay. When it came to videos, the quality was mediocre at best. That said, it's entirely possible that the quality of photos and videos directly correlated to the skill sets of the photographers, which were admittedly weak.

The main advantage of using our smartphones was convenience. It automatically geo-tagged and time stamped our content and then transferred it via Wi-Fi to our notebook. A few months into our trip, we decided that a better camera might help to compensate for our lack of skills. So, we did some research and decided to purchase a Panasonic Lumix DMC-ZS25 digital camera. We were greatly influenced by a review posted by a fellow world traveler and blogger at https://foxnomad.com. We found a good deal on the camera on Amazon and had it shipped to Elizabeth's parents, who then shipped it to us in a care package three months into the trip. We would have shipped it overseas, but Amazon didn't ship internationally at the time. We found this camera to take much better pictures and videos than our phones. It took better shots in low light and had a much better zoom lens. We were able to easily transfer images and video by removing the SD storage card and inserting it into our notebook.

Once the photos were transferred to our notebook, we used iPhoto to edit them. We know that there are much more sophisticated applications for this purpose, but iPhoto comes pre-loaded from Apple for free and it met our basic needs. We labeled the pictures that were worth keeping and deleted some that were not. We also organized them into albums by country, making it fairly easy to find a picture after the fact. We exported the pictures that we selected for the blog to a much smaller size to save disk space. We took approximately five thousand images on our trip. This seems like a lot, but when you average it out, that's only fifteen photos per day.

When it came to video, we uploaded all of the clips into iPhoto because it was easy and convenient to do so. However, once they were in iPhoto, there was not much that we could do with them other than watch them. We shot approximately one thousand video clips on our trip for an average of about three per day. Apple provides another free app called iMovie that can be used to edit them and produce a movie with a soundtrack in the background. iMovie is a much more sophisticated and powerful tool than iPhoto and took some effort to learn. Just as we started to get familiar with it, Apple issued a new version of the application. So, we upgraded in the hopes that it would make movie production easier. Unfortunately, the upgrade was so radical that we had to relearn how to use many basic features all over again. This was rather frustrating. Had we known what we were getting ourselves into, we would have stuck with the previous version.

When we look back at the movie clips we produced, the amateur result is all too apparent. The video quality clearly leaves something to be desired. Thankfully, we had the foresight to purchase a professional quality video of our bungy jump in New Zealand. When we went whitewater rafting on the Nile River in Uganda, the video offered for sale was too expensive for our tastes. However, the outfitter allowed the group in our raft to all chip in to buy and share a single copy of the photos, which we turned into a video. While producing the movies was fun, it was extremely time-consuming. This is due to our lack of skills, no doubt. On the bright side, it added another dimension to the wonderful memories that we preserved.

Our blog was a great way to keep family and friends abreast of our adventure. We decided that we wanted to have our own website domain name. We selected the name "ourtravelmenu" because it reflected our approach to travel and was available. We used iPage to register our domain name and to host our blog. To the best of our knowledge, iPage is not affiliated with Apple in any way. We selected Weebly Drag and Drop Builder as the tool to publish our blog posts. This tool had some limitations, and we switched over to WordPress near the end of the trip. We hired a freelancer named Yaroslav from Saint Petersburg, Russia, to help us migrate the site over for a modest fee. Coincidentally, when our travels took us through Saint Petersburg, we had the opportunity to meet Yaroslav in person and dine together at an authentic Russian restaurant. It was a great opportunity to discuss the blog and gain his insights into the local culture.

We had a few reasons in mind for writing the blog. First, we wanted to be able to keep family and friends, who were interested, informed of where we were and what we were up to. Second, we wanted it to serve as a resource for fellow travelers to gather information about a destination that they were interested in. We wanted to help others because we'd been helped so much by the various travel blogs that we'd read. Early in the trip, we developed a template to provide a framework for our blog posts that kept our writing focused and prevented us from rambling on about one topic or another. We also felt that by organizing each post in a similar fashion, readers could easily zero in on their interests. Finally, we selfishly wanted to preserve the memories of our trip for ourselves.

Writing the blog took more time and effort than we anticipated. Rich wrote the first draft. During the day, he jotted down observations or thoughts in the simple Notes app on his smartphone. In the evening, or perhaps in the morning as he was usually the first one up, he wrote content for the blog using Microsoft Word. He also imported the pictures, labeled them, and selected the ones that he felt were the best candidates for the upcoming blog post. He created a subfolder corresponding to each blog post to store the pictures in, simply inserting the picture's name in the Word document for reference. Once the draft was ready, Elizabeth edited the content. She provided Rich with some blunt constructive feedback on the first few posts (mainly that he was being too verbose). Once edited, Elizabeth used iPage and Weebly to prepare the content for publishing. She then turned it over to Rich to review and double-check that everything looked good. This is where he'd get to see what editing occurred. Upon completion of the final review, Elizabeth published the blog post to the live site. This whole process had the potential to cause some friction between us, but teaming up on the blog actually helped us become better collaborators. We have come to really value each other's constructive feedback and seek it out from each other. We also learned the lesson that two heads are better than one.

We wanted to map our trip to create a visual representation of where we'd been. We selected the free service provided by www.travellerspoint.com for this purpose. We came across this site when we were researching websites to host our travel blog. While we decided to go in a different direction for blog hosting, we found the site to be a valuable resource for travel information posted by fellow travelers and liked what we saw in the way of trip maps. Thus, we set one up and updated it with each new destination where we would be spending the night. We then embedded a link to the map on the home page of our blog. In addition to the map, the service provided some interesting statistics about the trip. In our case, we learned that we traveled well over 100,000 kilometers, which is the equivalent of circling the earth three times. We had no idea until we saw this fun fact on the Travellers Point site.

We also used Google's Calendar application to document our travel plans. This served several purposes. It allowed us to record where we were, where we were staying, where we were going next, and how we planned to get there. Whenever we booked lodging or transportation, we logged it in the calendar. We also identified how we booked and paid for each entry. For example, if we used frequent flier miles to pay for a flight, we made a note of it in the calendar. If we booked our room using a website such as www.booking.com, we noted that as well. We did this to provide additional insight into how we accomplished what we did.

We also used the calendar to forecast where we planned to travel to in the future, even if we hadn't booked the travel yet. We planned two to three weeks out, mostly as an aid for ourselves to search for travel deals on transportation and accommodations. Just as with our trip map, the home page of our blog included a link to our travel calendar. That way, family and friends could see what we were up to in real time. This was more reliable than our blog posts, which often lagged behind our travels by about a week or two.

If all of this seems like a lot of work, it was. But it was well worth it. We did it because we wanted to—not because we had to. It became a labor of love, and it helped to keep some of our communication and computer skills sharp. We hope that it will serve as a resource for other travelers and maybe even inspire others to take the plunge and embark on a trip of their own. Best of all, it preserved the memories of our journey for us to cherish forever.

Keeping In Touch

How will you keep in touch with family and friends back home? That depends on how accessible you want to be to them at any particular moment. Given how far away from home we would be, we felt that being connected 24–7 was unnecessary. We were frequently connected to the web, so if someone needed to get a hold of us in an emergency, we could respond within twenty-four hours. Our main reason for wanting to "disconnect" a little was that we wanted to take a break from texting and voice mails. Therefore, we made the decision before we left to cancel our domestic mobile phone service thereby forfeiting the mobile phone numbers that everyone knew us by. This was rather liberating. We had our providers unlock our phones so that we could use international SIM cards to access the

Internet and make phone calls. A couple of weeks into the trip, we decided to open a Skype account, which we used to make most of our phone calls back to the USA.

We started out with a pair of iPhones out of fear that if we ever got separated, then we'd still be able to get in touch with each other. In reality, we were almost never apart. When we were, it was usually because Rich was making a quick run to the store or café. As a result, Elizabeth rarely used her phone. We decided that it wasn't worth paying for service on it because she had her tablet as a backup with data service for Internet access. Thus, just three months into the trip, we decided to sell Elizabeth's phone. We found a good price offered by a reseller online. We mailed the phone to Elizabeth's parents from Hawaii, and they sent it off to the reseller in a pre-paid envelope provided by the reseller.

We equipped Rich's phone with an international SIM card from Telestial. While our research showed it to have the lowest rates of the generic international SIM cards on the market, we quickly found the cost for both calls and data to be much too high. In some cases, the cost was exorbitantly high. Fortunately, our exposure was limited to the $50 service credit that we'd pre-paid. Of course, technology is ever evolving and new solutions like www.gigsky.com are popping up that may offer more attractive solutions for you. So, keep your eyes open for the option that suits you best.

From that point forward, we decided to purchase a SIM card and service from a local mobile carrier when we arrived in each country. The initial cost ranged from $10 to $45 for both local phone service and data. The service included in each package varied dramatically from country to country and carrier to carrier. Talk time would vary from as little as five minutes up through unlimited service for thirty days. Data would vary from one hundred mega-bytes up through ten gigabytes. The duration of service also varied from seven to ninety days, with thirty days being the norm.

There was always an option to extend service beyond the initial term. The methods for doing so also varied. These methods included: right from the phone using a credit card, from our notebook via the Internet using a credit card, "topping up" at a convenience store or supermarket, and visiting a branch office belonging to the mobile carrier. Some carriers offered all of these options, while others offered only one of them. Many of the carriers' websites did not provide an English language version. When this occurred, we tried using Google's Chrome web browser to take advantage of its built-in language translation features. Sometimes it worked, and sometimes it didn't.

Obtaining a SIM card with data on it was important to us for several reasons. We relied on Google Maps for navigation, both when we were driving and walking. While we could pre-load the local maps to our phone via Wi-Fi, we needed cellular data service to obtain point-to-point directions. We also used various apps on our phone to search for places that we wanted to go to, such as a supermarket, restaurant, etc. These apps included: Google Maps, AroundMe, TripAdvisor, Yelp, Safari, etc. We also used the phone as a mobile hotspot while we were driving or in place of poor or nonexistent Wi-Fi where we were staying. In case you're unfamiliar with a mobile hotspot, it serves as a wireless router and enables you to use your mobile phone to connect other devices to the Internet. This was another lesson learned. Even though our phone had the ability to serve as a mobile hotspot, it didn't work unless the carrier supported it with its SIM card. We mistakenly assumed that as long as we had cellular data service on our phone, we could use our phone as a hotspot. However, this wasn't always the case. Thus, we learned to always inquire about support for this feature whenever we obtained a local SIM card.

Purchasing and activating a local SIM card often turned out to be an adventure. We found it best to try to do this when we arrived at an airport. We also learned that things went smoothest when we had the card installed and activated by the clerk who served us. These things were easier said than done. First, we didn't always arrive by plane. Second, several of the airports didn't have a kiosk to serve us. Third, there was the language barrier. When the clerk didn't speak English and there wasn't anything in English to describe the carrier's offerings, we found ourselves perplexed. Sometimes, we somehow overcame the obstacles, and sometimes we had to move on and wait until we could find a store in town.

We could relay lots of stories to you about what we went through to acquire a local SIM card, get it working, and get the correct amount of data that we'd paid for. The most memorable one occurred in Peru. We arrived at the airport late at night when everything was closed. The next day we noticed a kiosk in the front of a Lima supermarket for Claro, the mobile carrier that we preferred for Peru. We purchased a SIM card and asked to have it installed only to find that the kiosk only sold the SIM card, not service. The clerk sent us to a local convenience store to "top up" the card and obtain service. We did this and entered the code into the phone, but it didn't work. We returned to the supermarket to get assistance only to find that the kiosk was closed for siesta. Next, we located a Claro store in the area to get help, but the clerks there couldn't help us either. They sent us to a larger Claro store, where we waited in line until someone who spoke a little English was able to help us establish service. The whole process took about two hours out of our day. Experiences like this were not uncommon for us. In the end, however, we always got the service working, and we always got good use out of it. When we only intended to visit a country for a few days, we went without a local SIM card and just used our Telestial card if needed. We just made sure that we understood in advance what rates Telestial charged for the country before we made such decisions.

Do yourself a favor and open a Skype account before you leave for your trip. We did not do this, and it came back to haunt us later in the trip. When we were in Taiwan, we decided that it was time to open a Skype account. We expected this to be a simple process, but it was anything but that. For whatever reason, we could not gain access to the Skype site in the USA. We kept getting rerouted to the site in Taiwan, which did not have an English option. Google Chrome helped to translate much of the site but not all of it, and it was of no use when we got to the payments page. After much consternation, we purchased service to make unlimited calls from anywhere in the world back to the USA for just $60 for a full year.

We also used Skype on occasion to place calls to other countries related to our travel arrangements. These calls were deducted from credits that we pre-purchased. When we ran low on credits and needed to top up, we accessed Skype's website in English and navigated to what we needed, but when we went to purchase additional credits, we were redirected to a site in Taiwanese that we couldn't decipher. Attempts to use Skype customer service were exasperating because Skype does its darnedest to force customers to self-serve themselves to solve problems via forums on Skype's website. We had to jump through numerous hoops to gain access to a customer service rep, and even then, he or she was unable to solve the problem.

Luckily, Rich found a way to purchase more credit in English via Skype's mobile app, which he had installed on his phone.

We both enjoy reading and found the iPad mini to be versatile as both a Wi-Fi enabled device and eReader. We selected the Wi-Fi+cellular model compatible with ATT's service. We selected this model because our research showed that ATT offered international service that covered 150 countries. It wasn't cheap, but the price was fixed and when you ran out of data, the service stopped. Thus, we were protected from unknowingly running up a large cellular service bill. The ATT international data plan cost $30 for 128 MB that was good for thirty days or until you ran out. To get this plan, we were also required to have domestic data service in the USA, even though we'd never use it. The cheapest domestic data plan offering was 1 GB for three months for $25, which averages out to $8.33 per month. This brought our monthly cost to $38.

This came out to thirty cents per megabyte. Was it worth it? Yes, we used the tablet data quite a bit for directions on Google Maps and Internet access when we lacked Wi-Fi, such as when we were traveling by train. Somewhat surprisingly, the 128 MB usually covered our needs for the thirty-day period. Maybe that's because we used it sparingly and kept an eye on how much data we were using. We could see this in the "Cellular" tab under "Settings" on the tablet. At the beginning of each new cycle, we would "Reset Statistics" found at the very bottom of the "Cellular" section. This made it easy to keep track of our usage without the need to sign into our ATT account.

We started the trip with ATT service on each of our tablets. While this was nice to have, we found that we really only needed service on one tablet. After about three months, we decided to discontinue international data service on Rich's tablet. He still used his tablet with Wi-Fi and as an eReader, and he could always turn the data service back on if we felt the need. So, Rich carried the mobile phone, which usually had data service, and Elizabeth had data service on her tablet. Thus, we each had mobile data service on a device we were carrying, and we could use these devices to communicate with each other if we somehow got separated.

We found email to be a good form of communication with family and friends. This worked especially well given the big difference in time zones. We each have both Gmail and iCloud email accounts. Elizabeth is a fan of Facebook and uses it to stay in touch with family and friends. We found Facebook to be popular all over the world. However, she was unable to access it in China, where the government's firewalls block it. Fortunately, we found out how to get around this from a couple sitting next to us in a hostel lounge in Xi'an. They suggested that we install a VPN application, and it worked. Using VpnOneClick, Elizabeth was able to gain access to Facebook. We encountered this problem once again in another country but can't recall which one it was. Regardless, using a VPN service enabled us to successfully overcome it.

As for other mobile communications apps, we both have Twitter accounts but decided that providing frequent tweets regarding our trip would be overkill. We set up a Viber account with the thought that we'd use it to make free calls to friends and family over Wi-Fi, but we never used it. We also installed the popular WhatsApp at the request of Elizabeth's classmate and friend, Andrea. We used the app effectively to communicate with him regarding plans to meet in London, but we haven't used it since.

As you can see, we used several methods to communicate with

friends and family even when we were far, far away. In some cases, it took quite a bit of effort to get everything set up and working. When we take into account the costs for our Telestial SIM cards and service, iPad monthly ATT cellular service, Skype, local SIM cards and service for our mobile phone, and occasionally paying for Wi-Fi connectivity to the Internet, we probably averaged around $200 per month for such communication costs. This may seem like a lot, but it was definitely worth it to us.

Getting Along

A popular question that we've been asked upon our return is: How did you guys get along while spending so much time together? The answer is that we got along just fine. Hey, what can we say? We're compatible. We have common interests, with travel being one of them, and we were comfortable with a menu approach where we figured things out on the fly. Here are some insights into how we approached things that we think contributed to the harmony in our relationship on the road.

We made sure that we didn't bite off more than we could chew. We were okay if we didn't see everything that there was to see in each location. Far from it, we were content to get a feel for a new place and would try to catch just a few of the highlights. This put less pressure on us and took the stress out of sightseeing.

We have similar tastes in food. So, when we dined out, we liked to collaborate on what to order and then share our dishes with one another. This gave us more variety and made things more interesting. Collaborating on the selection of a wine was also a lot of fun.

Food wasn't the only thing that we shared. We divvied up responsibilities for travel planning as well. Each of us was primary for certain tasks. Rich was primary on transportation, visas, and pre-arrival scouting. (And while Elizabeth doesn't blame him, he takes full responsibility for dropping the ball on the Schengen Agreement, which led to our deportation.) Elizabeth was primary on lodging, where to eat, and sightseeing. Rich prepared the first draft of our travel blog posts. Elizabeth edited and published them.

This doesn't mean that we never crossed over to pitch in and help each other out. While Rich had transportation, Elizabeth figured out most of the trains and buses. While Elizabeth had lodging, Rich handled most of the hotel reward point bookings. Rich drove the rental cars, and Elizabeth navigated. We shared shopping, cooking, and laundry. The person who didn't cook took care of doing dishes and cleaning up. We guess you could say that it was a divide-and-conquer approach. By approaching things this way, there was never any build up of resentment that one of us was carrying more than his or her fair share of the load. We each got to be good at our own specialties, but two heads are better than one and we each picked each other up from time to time, which was always appreciated.

Homesick

Did we ever get homesick? The truthful answer is yes, but not often. While we missed family and friends from time to time, we communicated with them and still felt connected. That wasn't what made us homesick. Rather, there really is just no place like home. It's the cultural fit, the feeling of safety and security, the comfort foods, the sleeping in the same cozy bed, etc. Once in a while, we would long for these things. Like when we'd go out in the morning to get a coffee only to find that all of the coffee shops were closed, even the American branded coffee shops. How could that be? That would never happen back home. Or, when we'd go out for a late lunch only to find that all of the restaurants were closed for siesta. Are you kidding me? Back home, we could go out any time of the day and find something good to eat.

We also came to realize that we enjoy tremendous diversity in the USA. As an example, it's no secret that we love wine. During our trip, we found that wine selection was often limited to the nearby local wine-producing region. We didn't really mind this since we were usually excited to sample the local wines. However, occasionally we commented to one another how limited the selection was and that the locals didn't know what they were missing out on. One of the advantages of living in the USA is that we can readily obtain wines from all over the world.

We could continue on about the things that we missed, but you get the picture. Many people also asked us if we were sad when our trip was coming to an end? We can honestly say no. We were ready to return home to see our family and friends. Don't get us wrong, we enjoyed an amazing experience together that we'll cherish forever. We saw so many beautiful places and things all over the world. We learned so much about culture and history. And, last but not least, we gained a better appreciation for what we have in America. Our world travels made us grateful for the freedom and lifestyle that we enjoy in the USA. So yes, it's true, there's no place like home.

Key Ingredients

Staying Sane and Getting Along:

Entertainment:

- Consider bringing a tablet as an eReader and sign up with your local library before you leave so that you can borrow digital books and/or magazines to read as you please.

- Download a series or two of TV shows to one of your devices to enjoy on the road.
- Start a subscription to Netflix, Hulu, or a similar service and install a VPN service such as VpnOneClick so that you can still use the service in countries where it's not yet offered.
- Rent movies on one of your devices.
- Don't pay for HD quality when SD will do just fine. Save both money and disk space.
- Sign up for a music service, if you haven't already, to stream a wide variety of music.

Preserving Memories:

- Bring along a good camera with a decent zoom lens. The camera on your phone may suffice.
- Consider writing a blog to document your travels. If you plan to do this, make the necessary arrangements before you depart.
- Select a service to host your site, such as www.travellerspoint.com.
- Select a tool to edit and maintain your blog.
- Select a tool to edit and manage your photos and videos.
- Select an app on your mobile device to jot down notes during the day that you can later refer to when writing your blog entry.
- Consider using a service to document your travels on a world map that you can embed in your blog.
- Select a calendar application, such as Google's, to log your destinations and itineraries and embed that in your blog as well.

Keeping In Touch:

- Decide how connected and accessible you want to be during your trip.
- Contact your mobile carrier to unlock your mobile phones so that you can use local carriers' SIM cards.

- Turn your cellular data off on your mobile devices when you're not using the data so as not to incur unexpected data usage charges.
- Set up a Skype account before you leave so that you have unlimited calling back home at an affordable price.
- Consider enabling a tablet with an international mobile data plan.
- Make sure you scout out the quality of the Wi-Fi service before booking your lodging.
- Take precautions to protect your identity as best you can when using public computers to access the Internet. Clear the browser history and cache before logging off.

Getting Along:
- Pace yourself and don't bite off more than you can chew on your itinerary to reduce the stress of travel.
- Share the day-to-day responsibilities. Work together as a team.

Homesick:
- Expect to become homesick along the way. That's only natural. Hang in there and the feeling is likely to pass.

Dessert

Sweet Memories

Common Joy

Just as we put a stake in the ground to launch our trip, we decided to do the same thing to bring it to an end. We had started our trip in August and wanted to finish in August. We definitely wanted to go to Scotland in the summer, when it would be warm. So, in late spring, we started scouting out flights from Glasgow and Edinburgh to the USA using United miles that we had held in reserve for this very purpose. We found some flights that would work within our point balance, and we booked our return flights from Glasgow to New York City.

You may be wondering if we were sad to know that our trip was ending. Truth be told, we were looking forward to returning home to a place where we were familiar and to have the chance to see our family and friends again. We weren't in a rush, per se, but knowing that the trip would be coming to an end allowed us to really savor the time that we had left on the road, which we thoroughly did.

We were inspired by all of the beautiful places that we experienced during our journey. One evening as the sun was setting and we were admiring the view from our hotel balcony looking out over Lake Geneva in Switzerland, we put an entry on the menu for where we might live when we returned to the USA. We agreed that if it were possible, we would live in a place where we could enjoy the natural beauty of our surroundings. Luckily, we found such a place in Colorado, where we settled back down and where we were able to enjoy the majesty of the Rocky Mountains.

They say that the real joy of travel is found in retrospect by the lasting memories that are formed along the way. Some people jam so much activity into their trips that they don't really enjoy the trip itself, but they do enjoy the memories. We set a modest pace to really enjoy our travels while we were on the road. Now, we are happy to share our experiences with family and friends who express an interest and to serve as a resource for other travelers. And, yes, we're finding ourselves sharing fond memories of our travels with each other all the time. You could say that our trip has resulted in a common joy that we share. A similar common joy of wonderful travel memories is out there somewhere waiting for you and your partner to share.

We can honestly say that we have no regrets and would do it all over again. We lived a dream for a year, and it's back to reality for us. Now, it's your turn. If you're reading this book, you likely share our passion for travel. We're here to say that you too can live your travel dreams with your partner. Consider this book to be your recipe. Adapt it as you see fit. As the saying goes, "You only live once." So, what are you waiting for? Start compiling your list of exciting places to see and things to do. As our enthusiastic tour guide, Lady Zha Zha in Xi'an, China, would often say, "C'mon, let's go!"

Appendices

Appendix A

Scouting Matrix

Here is the list of information that we tried to capture for each country before our visit with an example for one country. Please do not rely on the information provided here because everything is subject to change over time and it's possible that we may have gotten something wrong. If you know what countries you plan to visit, you have the opportunity to fill it in before you leave. At the very least, please make sure that you understand the visa requirements before you depart so that there are no surprises and no disappointments. The "Pre-Arrival" chapter describes in detail how to find the information and create this matrix for your travels.

- Country: Taiwan.
- Visa required: No.
- Entry Fee: No.
- Airport Transportation: Bus (saved additional notes in phone to follow upon arrival).
- Currency: about 31 Taiwan New Dollar to one US dollar.
- ATM availability: Good.
- Credit Card Acceptance: Need cash for restaurants.
- Language: Taiwanese and Mandarin.

- Time zone: CST (G+8).
- Water drinkable? Yes.
- Local SIM card: None planned.
- Tipping guidelines: No. Service charge usually added to bill.
- Crime advisories: Low.
- Malaria Risks: None.
- Common Scams: None noted.
- Departure tax/fee: None.
- Food: Night markets are popular.
- Notes: None.

Appendix B

List of Possible Places to Visit

We suggest making a list of places you want to visit. You may not make it to all of them, but it's a good starting point and way to bring focus to your trip. Here is the initial list of places that we wanted to visit on our trip. Our focus was on quality not quantity. If you look through our blog (www.ourtravelmenu.com), you'll notice that we didn't make it to all of the places that we wanted to see, and we visited a couple of places that we originally planned to skip. We provide it as an example that you can model to create your own list.

Asia:
- China – Beijing (The Great Wall), Xi'an (Tombs of Emperors).
- Japan – Kyoto, sake.
- Hong Kong/Macau.
- Cambodia.
- Thailand – Avoid rainy season from June to November.
- India – Delhi, Taj Mahal.
- Singapore – The most popular time for visitors is June through July and November through December, when Singapore and most Southeast Asian countries have school holidays. The rest of the year is considerably quieter.

- Bali (Indonesia) – Borneo could be interesting, too.
- Sri Lanka.

Oceania:
- Australia – Perth and Margaret River.
- New Zealand – Milford Sound and fjords, Milford Track.

South America:
- Argentina.
- Chile.
- Galápagos Islands (Ecuador).
- Peru (Machu Picchu).
- Venezuela – Angel Falls, highest in world plunging 3,212 feet.

Africa:
- South Africa – Cape Town, wines: chenin blanc, vin de Constance, pinotage.
- Zambia – Victoria Falls, a must-see but security/safety is a concern.
- Morocco.
- Malawi.
- Botswana? – Expensive but productive safaris.
- Ghana.

Middle East:
- Israel.
- Jordan.
- U.A.E. Dubai.

Europe:
- Austria.
- France – Bordeaux, Loire Valley, Champagne, Normandy.
- Czech Republic – Prague, Bohemia.
- Gibraltar (The Rock of…).
- Hungary – Budapest.

- Iceland.
- Italy – Rome, Coliseum, Sicily.
- Portugal.
- Scotland – hiking the highlands (Ben Nevis, highest point in UK).
- Switzerland.
- Greenland.

Appendix C

Clothing List

Here is a list of what each of us packed for the trip. We didn't receive any endorsements for the brands we bought. We tried on everything before we committed to bringing them and shopped at stores that were accessible to us at the time and that stocked a lot of great travel gear, such as REI and Paragon Sports.

We didn't bring anything for really cold weather, so when we got to Ushuaia, Argentina, we ended up buying some inexpensive fleece jackets, scarves, gloves, and hats to make it through the cold. Once we reached a warmer climate, we donated our clothes to a local charity.

Rich

Clothes:

1 Short-sleeve, soft cotton shirt (Kenneth Cole blue)

2 Short-sleeve, quick-dry T-shirts (Under Armour gray, Columbia High and Dry Cinabar): *These served as everyday shirts that blended in with most cultures.*

1 Long-sleeve, cotton T-shirt (Banana Republic gray): *For keeping warm and being comfortable in transit.*

1 Long-sleeve, button-down shirt (Columbia Omni Shade

SPF30 blue plaid): *A "dressier" option. Rich added another long-sleeve shirt (K-Way khaki) in Africa for our safari.*

1 Short-sleeve polo shirt (Callaway light blue dri-fit): *A less formal but still dressy option.*

1 Workout T-shirt (Nike blue dri-fit): *For runs/hitting the gym.*

2 Sleeping/undershirts (Uniqlo Airism gray and Uniqlo blue)

1 Jacket, rain- and wind-repellent (Marmot Aegis Jacket gray): *Worn infrequently but invaluable when needed.*

1 Pair of pants (ExOfficio Men's Kukura Trek'r Pants in gray): *A nicer option for dressing up and keeping warm.*

1 Pair of pants, convertible to shorts, UV protection and bug-repellent (ExOfficio Men's Bugsaway Ziwa Collection Convertible Pants in khaki): *Great for trekking when the weather changes.*

1 Pair of shorts (ExOfficio Men's Kukura Trek'r Shorts in gray): *Nice shorts option from the khaki convertibles.*

1 Pair of workout shorts/swimsuit (Nike gray dri-fit): *Handy for the gym and the pool.*

1 Money belt (Tom Bihn): *This was a great and inconspicuous precaution against pickpocketing. Rich carried several US $100 bills and paper copies of our passports and major visas wrapped in resealable plastic sandwich bags, which protected the contents from perspiration.*

5 Pairs of undershorts (3 ExOfficio and 2 Uniqlo): *Lightweight, breathable, and quick drying.*

3 Pairs of short socks (Smartwool: 1 PhD Running Light Micro Crew and 2 PhD Ultra Light Micro Crew): *Smartwool is one of our favorite brands for both staying warm and keeping cool.*

2 Pairs of long socks (Smartwool Cozy)

Shoes:

Keen Turia sandals: *Super-lightweight and great for everyday walking and long day hikes.*

Saucony Type A5 running shoes: *Lightweight and breathable.*

Toiletries—many of these were shared:

Glasses, contact lenses, contact lens case, contact lens solution (2-ounce x 3 to start; switched to 4-ounce x 2 during the trip)

Razor and blades

Deodorant: *Solid so that it wasn't restricted with liquids for air travel.*

Toothbrush with plastic end cap

Toothpaste

Dental floss

Nail clippers

Battery-powered razor

Medicine:

Malaria pills

Imodium

Vitamins: Multi and D

Allergy

Advil

Excedrin

Prescriptions

Everything Else:

MacBook Air with BackBlaze backup subscription over Wi-Fi in the cloud

iPad Mini with ATT International Data Plan and Telestial

International Data SIM card as a backup

iPhone unlocked with Telestial Passport Lite International SIM Card

iPod and earbuds

Power cords: iMac, iPad Mini, iPhone/iPod Shuffle

USB Car charger (cigarette lighter attachment): *Google Maps is a power hog, and this came in really handy when we rented cars*

International power plug converter

Eye shades and ear plugs

Sunglasses

Compression bag to efficiently store jacket when not needed

Plastic shopping bag

Ziploc bags, varying sizes

Rubber bands: *These were especially handy to keep snack bags closed*

2 Elastic clotheslines for drying

Corkscrew: *Think plastic; we wish we had from the very beginning*

Towel (Microfiber Travel)

Laundry soap bar (Fels-Naptha)

Sink drain plug for laundry

Travel lock for backpack (Master Cable TSA 3 dial)

Daypack (Patagonia Lightweight Travel Pack)

Health insurance (GeoBlue High Deductible International Health Insurance)

Elizabeth

Clothes:

3 Short-sleeve, quick-dry T-shirts (Columbia UV Shirt in blue, Under Armour black stripe, Nike blue): *Great everyday shirts for trekking and working out*

1 Eastern Mountain Sports long-sleeve T-shirt

1 Short-sleeve, cotton T-shirt (Under Armour pink): *Super-comfy and attractive*

1 Short-sleeve, quick-dry collared shirt (Columbia in green): *For something a little dressier*

2 Cardigans (Banana Republic in black, Wrap Cardigan in blue): *I kept these handy for temp changes*

3 Pairs of Smartwool long hiking socks

2 Pairs of Smartwool short running socks

1 Jacket, rain- and wind-repellent (Marmot)

1 Horny Toad black skirt: *This was really comfortable and easy to pair with any top*

1 Horny Toad black dress: *This served as my dressy option*

1 ExOfficio Columbia tan convertible pants: *Worked great for changing climates*

1 ExOfficio 3/4 water wicking pants: *A good option when you need something to cover your knees*

5 Pairs of ExOfficio wicking underwear

1 Pair of cotton sleep shorts from JCPenney

1 Nike tankini 2-piece bathing suit

Shoes:

Merrell Protera Vim Sport, replaced by Keen Newport H2 hiking sandals during the trip

Saucony Kinvara 4 lightweight running shoes

Crocs sandals/flip-flops

Everything Else:

iPad Mini with ATT International Data Plan and Telestial

International Data SIM card as a backup

iPhone unlocked with Telestial Passport Lite International SIM Card

iPod Shuffle and headphones

International power converter

Toothbrush with plastic end cap

Eye shades and ear plugs

Sunglasses

Hair brush

Compression bag to efficiently store jacket when not needed

2 Plastic shopping bags

Ziploc Bags, varying sizes

Towel (Microfiber Travel)

Travel lock for backpack (Master Cable TSA 3 dial)

Backup pair of eyeglasses and contact lens case for Rich

Daypack (Patagonia Lightweight Travel Sling)

OurTravelMenu business cards

Health Insurance (GeoBlue High Deductible International Health Insurance)

Additional items that we added along the way:

2 Sturdy small wineglasses with protective bubble-wrap sleeves

1 Comb

1 Digital camera, charger and 32GB Micro SIM Card (Panasonic Lumix DMC-ZS25 16.1 MP w/20X Zoom)

SIM card in each country, usually from top mobile carrier for talk time and data

Mini hair drier

Muscle shirt to stay cool for Rich

Tank Tops for Elizabeth to stay cool

Pocket tissues

Hand sanitizer

Appendix D

Final Details Checklist

Here is a generic copy of the checklist that we used to take care of all of the final details. We provide it as a starting point for you to modify and customize to help ensure that you haven't forgotten anything.

- Build up travel fund kitty – log total contribution, joint bank account balance and brokerage account balance.
- Obtain necessary visas.
- Scan critical documents and store them in the cloud and email them to yourself as appropriate.
    - For example: visas, passports, driver's licenses, credit & debit cards, bank account check images, income tax records, etc.
- Make paper copies of passports & visas to take with you.
- Log replacement details: such as prescription numbers, contact lenses, etc.
- Start a cloud backup service such as Backblaze for your laptop computer(s).
- Tighten up identity theft security of financial account user names and passwords as you'll be relying on them for your funds.

- Archive all photos off of mobile phones onto DVD and/or the cloud.
- Buy language translation pocketbook(s) and/or mobile phone Apps such as iTranslate.
- File change of address form with USPS.
- Set up a blog.
- Create business cards to share contact info with new acquaintances you meet.
- Wedding bands – buy inexpensive replacements and store originals in safe deposit box.
- Obtain necessary shots such as yellow fever and obtain an Immunization International Certificate.
- Health insurance – obtain international coverage – We selected Geo Blue with a $2,500 deductible.
- Purchase Telestial Passport Lite SIM card or similar as safety net for mobile data.
- Purchase ATT's global data plan or similar for tablet(s).
- Unlock mobile phone(s) – Call your carrier to ensure your phone is unlocked.
- Cancel utilities and Internet service provider.
- Turn in any rental equipment such as a cable modem or router.
- Turn in any employee equipment, access cards, etc. to your employer(s).
- Cancel domestic wireless carrier service.
- Put valuables in safe deposit box and log where keys are stored.
- Use www.craigslist.org to sell remaining items such as furniture.
- Update LinkedIn profile page(s).

- Cancel EZ-Pass electronic toll payment.
- Cancel auto insurance.
- Cancel apartment insurance.
- Credit & debit cards – make sure there are no foreign transaction fees on the ones you'll use and that they're enabled for international charges and won't expire while you're away; store images and info in the cloud.
- Call debit & credit card companies to notify them of your extended travel plans.
- Turn keys in to management office on the morning that you leave.
- Print directions in the local language to your initial accommodations.

Appendix E

Credit and Debit Card Tracker

Here's a list of the information that you should keep track of for each of your credit and debit cards. We created a simple spreadsheet; password-protected it, and stored it in the cloud. It will come in handy if one or more of your cards is lost or stolen and needs to be reported and replaced.

- Primary cardholder's name.
- Card name (i.e., name of card issuer and card type).
- Account number.
- Security code (3 digits for most card types and 4 characters for American Express cards).
- Expiration date.
- Annual fee.
- Renewal date.
- US phone number (usually found on the back of the card).
- International call collect phone number (usually found on the back of the card).
- Credit limit.
- Foreign transaction fee (none or enter the percentage that applies).

Appendix F

Reward Points Tracker

Here's a list of the information that you should keep track of for all of your Reward Program Points earned. We created a simple spreadsheet; password-protected it, and stored it in the cloud. We recommend that you update your balances as you use your points during your trip.

- Program name.
- Account number.
- User ID.
- Password.
- Points/miles balance.
- Notes.

Appendix G

SIM Card Tracker

Here's a list of the information that you need to keep track of all of your SIM cards. We used this to keep track of our international Telestial SIM cards. We created a simple spreadsheet; password-protected it, and stored it in the cloud. We recommend that you update your balances from time to time so that you don't run out of data or minutes when you need them.

- Carrier name.
- Card type.
- Device (that it will be used in).
- Global phone number (if applicable).
- US phone number (if applicable).
- PIN.
- PUK (PIN Unlock Key).
- Website URL to reload credit.
- Balance.
- Date when balance was logged.
- Notes.

Appendix H

Helpful Apps and Websites

We mention numerous apps and websites that we used on our mobile devices throughout the book. Here's a consolidated list for easy reference:

- 8 Tracks.
- AccuWeather.
- BackBlaze to backup our MacBook Air with access from our mobile phone.
- Chrome, especially for translation capabilities.
- Compass.
- Digital library book loans from library back home to gain temporary access to travel guides like Lonely Planet.
- Facebook.
- Google Calendar to let friends and family know where we'd be.
- Google Maps and occasionally Apple Maps.
- iBooks and Kindle for iPad.
- iMovie to produce our videos.
- iPhone Alarm clock.
- iPhoto to manage our photos.

- iTranslate to communicate in a foreign language.
- iTunes to store and play our music, rent movies and TV shows.
- Netflix and VpnOneClick (so that we could still watch Netflix in countries that don't have it).
- Reminders.
- Simply Noise for white noise to help us sleep.
- Skype: We purchased a low-cost annual subscription that enabled us to make unlimited calls to the USA.
- TripAdvisor for reviews and things to do.
- Wallet to hold our boarding passes.
- www.agoda.com for lodging.
- www.airbnb.com for lodging.
- www.booking.com for lodging.
- www.hotels.com for lodging.
- www.iPage.com and www.wordpress.org to write our blog.
- www.seat61.com to plan travel by train.
- www.skyscanner.com to search for airfare deals.
- www.travellerspoint.com to map our trip.
- www.vrbo.com for lodging.
- www.wikitravel.org and www.wikivoyage.org.
- www.xe.com and Xe app for currency exchange.

Index

CPSIA information can be obtained
at www.ICGtesting.com
Printed in the USA
FSHW02n0811200918
52198FS